A NEW THERAPY FOR POLITICS?

A NEW THERAPY FOR POLITICS?

Andrew Samuels

KARNAC

First published in 2015 by
Karnac Books Ltd
118 Finchley Road
London NW3 5HT

British Library Cataloguing in Publication Data

A C.I.P. for this book is available from the British Library

ISBN-13: 978-1-78220-317-9

Typeset by V Publishing Solutions Pvt Ltd., Chennai, India

Printed in Great Britain

www.karnacbooks.com

For Sissy

CONTENTS

ACKNOWLEDGEMENTS

Writing is far from being a solitary activity and I could not have written the book without input and feedback from: Henry Abramovitch, Neil Altman, Helena Bassil-Morozow, John Beebe, Jessica Benjamin, Muriel Dimen, Jimmy Fisher, Chris Hauke, Gottfried Heuer, Irwin Hoffman, Richard House, Tom Kirsch Lynne Layton, Del Loewenthal, Kevin Lu, Sissy Lykou, Susie Orbach, Renos Papadopoulos, Tom Singer, David Tacey, Nick Totton, Luigi Zoja, and members of the e-mail discussion lists of the International Association for Jungian Studies and of The Relational School (London). Some of these folk have been on the journey for decades, and I thank everyone. The responsibility for the contents is, of course, mine.

I would also like to thank the Karnac team for their efficiency and encouragement. Having first published with the company in 1989, and been associated with it in other ways, I can testify to the huge creative developments that have taken place in its publishing business. I want to acknowledge: Cecily Blench, Nick Downing, Constance Govindin, Oliver Rathbone, and Rod Tweedy (my editor).

Permission to utilise my own work is gratefully acknowledged: to John Wiley & Sons, Ltd, for material which first appeared in *Psychotherapy and Politics International* (12:2, 2014, pp. 99–110) as "Appraising the role of the individual in political and social change processes: Jung, Camus, and the question of personal responsibility—possibilities and impossibilities of making a difference", and as "A new anatomy of spirituality: clinical and political demands the therapist cannot ignore" (2:3, 2006, pp. 201–211). To Routledge, for material first published in *The Political Psyche* (London and New York, 1993). Permission to include the untitled poem by Jerzy Ficowski from *Holocaust Poetry* © 1995 edited by Hilda Schiff has been gratefully received from St. Martin's Press. All rights reserved.

ABOUT THE AUTHOR

Andrew Samuels is recognised internationally as a leading commentator from a psychotherapeutic perspective on political and social problems. His work on the father, sexuality, spirituality, and transference-countertransference has also been widely appreciated. He was co-founder of Psychotherapists and Counsellors for Social Responsibility and chair of the UK Council for Psychotherapy. He is Professor of Analytical Psychology at Essex University and holds visiting chairs at New York, London, Roehampton, and Macau Universities.

His many books have been translated into nineteen languages, including *Jung and the Post-Jungians* (Routledge, 1985); *A Critical Dictionary of Jungian Analysis* (Routledge, 1986); *The Father* (New York, 1986); *The Plural Psyche: Personality, Morality and the Father* (Routledge, 1989); *Psychopathology* (Karnac, 1989); *The Political Psyche* (Routledge, 1993); *Politics on the Couch* (Karnac, 2001); *Relational Psychotherapy, Psychoanalysis and Counselling: Appraisals and Reappraisals* (edited with Del Loewenthal, Routledge, 2014); and *Persons, Passions, Psychotherapy, Politics* (Routledge, 2014). His lectures and "rants" are on: www.andrewsamuels.com

INTRODUCTION

This book depends on the making of plausible links between social and political phenomena and psychotherapy. Although the field can often be seen as consisting of the application of the latter to the former, all my writing has deployed a two-way street approach, so that the social dimension may critique, illumine, and transform the psychological. For psychological experience and social life are fundamentally entangled with each other. Psychological issues and subjective experiences cannot be abstracted from societal, cultural, and historical contexts. But they cannot be deterministically reduced to the social. Similarly, social and cultural worlds have psychological dimensions and are shaped by psychic processes and intersubjective relations.

A main purpose of the book is to assess the contribution of psychotherapy to stopping us from thinking like the state wants us to think. To do this requires some recalibration of the profession's overall political stance. There was a quality of radical mind that, as many have noted, seems to have been present in the beginnings of the profession of psychotherapy but was subsequently lost in the pursuit of acceptance by the powerful. I hope the chapters convey in some small measure how this foundational radicalism may be recuperated, in part by adopting a wide definition of "politics".

I am a practising psychotherapist as well as being an academic (and a political activist). I have been careful to test out the limitations of the project of this book. Yes, enthusiasm—but also scepticism and caution.

I wanted to write a book that incorporated methodological innovation. Previously, I had worked out how contemporary thinking about the therapist's subjective experience and countertransference could be reworked into a way in which individual citizens might perform political and social critique. In this book, I have made the experiential dimension explicit by asking the reader(s) to join in carefully constructed and tested experiential exercises—individually, in pairs, and in groups.

But there are also palpable "issues" being addressed beyond subjective experience: aggression and violence, leadership, economics, environmentalism/nature, the question of an individual "making a difference" in political struggle, promiscuity as a socio-political matter, spirituality in social context, fundamentalism, the father in society, what we mean by "the child", and anti-Semitism.

To be honest, the possible contribution of psychotherapy to society beyond the alleviation of individual distress has not been much welcomed. The world did not show up for its first session. Even clinical work with individuals has been castigated as the new opium for the masses, diverting attention from social ills and fostering a false independence that scorns the virtues of communal life.

Frankly, we psychotherapists have brought this set of frustrations upon ourselves. Too often, we are more concerned to prove our theoretical perspectives correct rather than struggle for changes on the ground. The maddening rectitude of the psychotherapist allies with a mindless reductionism in which every social phenomenon is treated as if it were nothing but a psychic fragment—an unappealing pan-psychism.

Then there is the bad record of psychotherapy with regard to difference and diversity of all kinds, especially with regard to sexual minorities. Even now, when homophobia is banished, there is a tendency in the therapy world to divide people into "good gays" and "bad gays". The former ape what are claimed to be the merits of long-term heterosexual relationships and marriage. The latter are regarded as behavioural provocateurs and thoughtlessly promiscuous.

Then people outside the field have to understand how incredibly difficult it is to access psychotherapy, unless you are pretty wealthy, other than a particularly mechanistic kind of state therapy. It is equally difficult for members of ethnic minorities or working class people to train as psychotherapists. These difficulties cover a wide range of concerns including the high cost of training, the Eurocentric cast of the ideas and concepts being taught, and the bourgeois and "polite" atmosphere of many training institutes.

Last in this sin list, there is the appalling historical record of dispute and mutual "dissing" between the various schools of psychotherapy. If our professional politics are so horrible, how on earth can we expect to be welcomed as potential contributors to political discourse and process "out there"?

The philosopher's stone remains the successful and widespread application of psychotherapeutic ideas in an interdisciplinary quest for deeper understandings of social and political processes and problems—such as the superficiality and inequity of contemporary life, or the seeming ineradicability of war and violence, or perplexing collective phenomena such as climate change denial.

The problem is what we mean by "application". If we mean an interpretation from on high of what is happening done in psychotherapy's own terms, then many will find it distasteful. This is what the problem of reductionism I mentioned earlier means in practice. The great skill of psychotherapists is to be both a little outside what they are being told by the client—and also deeply in it as well. This desideratum applies also when attempting to "analyse the culture".

I am careful about tracing off from psychological ideas developed in the context of individual work. But I would like to mention a few of such ideas that I deploy in the book:

- good-enoughness (but in a political and not a familial setting)
- sadism and the shadow (in relation to prospects for economic equality)
- the definitions developed within psychotherapy of an "individual"
- the communicative functions and potentials of the body.

Finally, a note on the activist-therapist. Social and political projects carried out by groups of psychotherapists remain very interesting. We have seen the formation in the mid-90s of Psychotherapists and Counsellors for Social Responsibility and there have been specific issue groups concerned with nuclear weapons and climate change/sustainability. Yet it has to be said that, for many psychotherapists, the question of how to blend activism with their role and persona as professional clinicians remains a problem.

CHAPTER ONE

Therapy thinking and political process— possibilities and limitations

As Robert Musil put it, "I am convinced not only that what I say is wrong, but that what will be said against it will be wrong as well. Nonetheless, a beginning must be made; for the truth is to be found not in the middle of such a subject but around the outside, like a sack which changes shape every time a new opinion is stuffed in, but grows firmer all the while" (Musil, 1990, p. 167).

The intention in this first chapter is to test out and explore the boundaries that we have been told exist between therapy and politics, between the inner world and the outer world, between being and doing, and even between what many people still cannot resist calling "feminine" approaches to life and "masculine" approaches to life—no matter how problematic those words are.

I begin by addressing the questions "Why me, why here, why now?" Then there follows a discussion of how politics in the West is changing in the direction of what I call "transformative politics". Third, I ask the question "Can therapists really make a difference in the world today?" Fourth, there is a markedly experiential section entitled "the inner politician". Finally, to conclude, there are a few reflections on the relationship between psychotherapy and politics.

Why me, why here, why now?

The bases for these ideas about therapy thinking and political process do not only lie in my experience as a clinical practitioner. They stem from my involvement as a consultant with politicians, parties, and activist groups in several counties. I have also conducted workshops with members of the public in many places across the world. These activities have given me an indication of how useful and effective perspectives derived from psychotherapy might be in the formation of policy in creating new ways of thinking about the political process, and in the resolution of conflict. It is difficult to present therapy thinking so that mainstream politicians—for example, a US Presidential candidate or a senior Democrat Senator or a Labour Party committee—will take it seriously. And the problem is only slightly reduced when the politicians and organisations are "alternative" or more activist.

Many have written that politics in Western countries is broken and in a mess; we urgently need new ideas and approaches. Psychotherapists, alongside economists, social scientists, religious people, environmentalists, and others, can contribute to a general transformation of politics. Today's politicians leave many people with a visceral sense of deep despair and disgust; this reaction may have been present for a long time but it seems to have intensified in the twenty-first century. The politicians lack integrity, imagination, and new ideas. Across the globe, and in response to the challenge, a search is on to remodel politics. Psychotherapy's contribution to this search depends on opening up a two-way psychosocial street between inner realities and the world of politics. We need to balance attempts to understand the secret politics of the inner world of emotional, personal, and family experiences with the secret psychology of pressing outer world matters such as leadership, the economy, environmentalism, nationalism, and war.

Our inner worlds and our private lives reel from the impact of policy decisions and the existing political culture. Why, then, do our policy committees and commissions not have a psychotherapist sitting on them as part of a range of experts? This is not a call for a committee of therapists! But just as a committee will often have a statistician present, whose role might not be fully enjoyed by the other members, so, too, there should be a therapist at the conference table. We would expect to find therapists having views to offer on social issues that involve personal and familial relationships or matters to do with mental health but they may also have ideas to contribute on the "hard" issues as well—war, violence, poverty, and the economy.

Is it possible to imagine a world in which people are encouraged to sharpen their half-thought out, intuitive political ideas and commitments so as to be able to take more effective political action as and when they want to? There are probably buried sources of political wisdom in many people, particularly those who do not seem likely to function in such a way. More and more, I look to introverted people, the shy or ashamed ones, to poets and mystics, to unprivileged voices, to the older generation who seem to get angrier about the state of the world rather than more accepting of it, and those whose attitude to politics is to avoid involvement—these individuals may know much that the more active, talkative, educated, and lucky among us do not. They are a great aid in finding out how secret things, such as childhood experiences, intimate relationships, fantasies (including sexual fantasies), dreams, and bodily sensations, might be reframed and turned to useful political ends.

Thinking about those who usually do not say much, I find that they make a profound contribution to what I call "political clinics". These are large group events, often composed of people who have nothing to do with therapy and psychology at all, but who come together to explore their emotional and feelings-based reactions to major political themes such as terrorism, the Middle East, racism, homelessness, surveillance (to give a few examples). I have discovered that people who say "I am not interested in politics" are often deceiving themselves, caught in a reaction formation. Then it becomes clear, as the event unfolds, that they are indeed extremely interested, knowledgeable, and wise about politics, but have always doubted, because they have been taught to doubt, that the inward emotional reactions they are having are a legitimate part of political process. We have educated our peoples in the Western countries, not to *deny* that they have emotions about politics, because that would be impossible, but to put those emotions rather low down on the scale of what we value in official political debate and political discussion.

Sometimes, at the conclusion of these political clinics, we start to talk in terms of citizens as "therapists of the world" who have a large set of usable countertransferences to the political culture in which they live. This constitutes an intellectual challenge to much psychological theorising about citizens, especially in psychoanalysis, wherein the citizen is regarded as a kind of baby, who has a transference and a collection of fantasies towards the "parental" society in which she or he lives. Flipping that round, so that the citizen is seen as a kind of therapist or parent figure towards the society, can have a radical, uplifting, and empowering effect. It overturns the tradition, especially in psychoanalysis (e.g., Richards, 1984), in which the citizen is seen as the baby and society as the parent. This claim, that the citizen is capable of being the therapist (or the parent) of the world is one that embodies many possibilities as we struggle to work out what citizens are "for" when their voices are distorted by the mass media, and what their internal life will be in a highly fraught political climate dominated by corporations and cartels.

Transformative politics

We move on now to the second section of the chapter, which is about how politics is slowly changing in Western countries. We are at a very interesting moment in political consciousness. What used to be an elitist insight about how everything is secretly political is now on the verge of becoming an element in mass awareness. For years now, feminists, academics, intellectuals, some therapists and analysts have lived happily with the idea that the personal, psychological, and private worlds of individuals are full of collective political tensions, dynamics, and energies. But actually this has been a superior form of knowing, a political Gnosticism. So "we" intellectuals and academics knew that politics has expanded its definition to include all the private stuff. But the people, the masses, did not. They continued to be taught, but now accept it less, that politics means official politics, party-politics, congressional or parliamentary politics, power politics, the politics that money can buy, and so on. What has helped to accelerate the democratisation of the personal-is-political insight has been the huge eruptions of feelings over certain events in recent years. A level of affect is achieved that turns mere events into what can justly be called archetypal or at least numinous experiences: 9/11, the reaction to Princess Diana's death, natural disasters. The most ruthlessly successful politicians of recent times, such as Tony Blair, have perceived this move into general awareness of the elitist, Gnostic, private knowledge about how politics has changed and hence have decided to couch their utterances in the language of the emotions. How sincere they are about this is a moot point.

Another way in which politics has changed is that it has become more of a transformative process. By this I mean that engagement in political activity and processes of personal growth and development are seen increasingly as the same thing or at least two sides of a coin. If one interviews people active in anti-capitalist politics, or in the sustainable development/climate change/environmental movements, or in certain sectors of feminism and the men's movements, or in ethnopolitics, one sees that what they are doing is, in many respects, a form of self-healing that is familiar to psychotherapists. So politics starts to carry an overtly psychological, transformative burden. Sadly, this kind of transformative politics is not only progressive and left-leaning, it can also be spotted in many right-wing and reactionary movements.

A third way in which politics has changed is that there is now something which could be called "political energy" to be considered alongside political power. Political power is what you would imagine it is. It is control over resources, such as land, or water, or oil—or indeed, information and imagery. Especially today, the issue of who controls information and imagery, for example on the Internet and satellite television, is almost as important as the issue of who controls oil or water. Political power is held by the people you would expect to hold it: men, white people, the middle and upper-middle classes, and those who run the big institutions of finance, the military, and the academic and professional worlds, including the world of mental health.

Political energy is different. It is almost the opposite of political power. Political energy involves idealism and an imaginative and visionary focus on certain political problems with a view to making a creative impact in relation to those problems (not necessarily with the goal of "solving" them). Political energy seeks out more political energy in an attempt to build up to critical mass. It is different from political power because people who have political energy, imagination, commitment, idealism, real compassion, almost by definition lack political power. And, equally, almost by definition in contemporary societies, people who have political power tend to lack political energy. This is a fundamental and radical claim that I am sure will be much disputed.

Indeed, the very idea of political energy will upset some intellectual apple carts, for most academics cannot entertain the notion. Energy does not exist they say; it is only a mechanistic nineteenth-century way of looking at things. Be that as it may, Jung suggested that, *contra*

Freud's conception of libido, there was a neutral form of psychic energy that could run down various "channels", citing biological, psychological, spiritual, and moral channels. My proposal is that there is also a social channel and that a subset of the social channel will have to do with politics and political energy. Hence, I use the term "energy" in both a metaphorical and a literal sense.

Jung's further idea that there is a specifically moral channel for psychic energy is extremely interesting, chiming with much evolutionary, ethological, genetic, and psychoanalytic thought—Klein's idea of an innate superego, Winnicott's insistence that children have an inborn sense of guilt and hence are not born amoral, Milner's counsel that we stop seeing morality solely as something implanted in children by parents and society. Freud foreshadowed this train of thought with his remarks about the innate disposition of the self-preservative instincts to become more socially oriented (Freud, 1905, p. 176). (See Samuels, 1989, pp. 194–215 for a fuller discussion of "original morality".)

People with political energy are doing something rather new and different in the Western world today compared to what those with political power are doing. This thought can be liberatory if you are working in a small neighbourhood group, or a social and political project with limited resources and support, or alongside people who have been abused, or trying to build up an environmentally informed movement for sustainable development and worldwide economic justice. If you are doing any or all of these things then you probably do not have much power. It is very easy then to judge yourself the way the conventional political world might judge you—as a waste of space when it comes to "real" politics.

But the very notion of political energy is intended to shift this way of thinking. Very often when I talk about this, people say "Yes, and we wonder what would happen if our country valued political energy as much as it values political power". If political energy is not to be found in the sites of official politics, then where may we find it? Politics has left its home base and gone out into the world to redefine itself and find other and new places to settle. I am not *advocating* removing political energy from moribund formal institutions; this has been happening in Western societies anyway over many years in one of the most significant sociocultural and collective psychological shifts to take place in the developed countries since the end of the Second World War. A striking feature of the past thirty years in such societies has been the spontaneous growth of new social and cultural networks. More and more people are now involved in these networks—increasingly aware that what they are doing may be regarded as political. The contemporary elasticity in our definition of politics is not something that has been worked out by intellectuals. Nor has there been a concerted effort to achieve such a shift, for the new social movements operate in isolation from each other. Yet they have something psychological in common. They share in an emotional rejection of "big" politics, its pomposity and self-interest, its mendacity and complacency. They share a *Weltanschauung* and set of values based on ideas of living an intelligible and purposeful life in spite of the massive social and financial forces that mitigate against intelligibility and purpose. Such social movements include environmentalism, groups working for the rights of ethnic and sexual minorities, animal liberation, complementary medicine, spiritual and religious groups including paganism and neo-paganism, rock and other kinds of music and art, finding God in the new physics, sports, organic farming—and psychoanalysis, psychotherapy, and counselling.

At one point (Samuels, 1993), I referred to the social movements as participating in a "rescralisation" of politics. "Sacral" means holy, and the intent was to pick up on the attempt to get a sense of purpose, decency, aspiration, and meaning back into political culture. When I considered attempts by analysts and psychotherapists to do their bit, I have no alternative but to count them as part of this general, worldwide resacralising movement. So, too, the relatively new academic discipline of psychosocial studies. Psychotherapists and academics may want to be different and special but in their attempts to work the borders between psychotherapy and society they are part of something bigger, even if the rhetoric sometimes feels too "New Age-y".

Psychotherapists tend to share with other resacralisers a sense of disgust with present politics and politicians. In political clinics, this is often a literal and physical disgust, involving the gagging reflex, an ancient part of the nervous system, absolutely necessary for survival in a world full of literal and metaphorical toxins.

Let me conclude this section by accepting that a transformation of politics is not going to happen in any kind of simple or speedy way and may not happen at all. There is an impossibility to the whole project because the social realm is as inherently uncontrollable as the drives and images of the inner world and the unconscious. Once human desire enters into a social system—as it always will—that system cannot function predictably (I return to this theme in Chapter Three, on economics). There are no final solutions to social questions. The social issues which face Western societies are as incorrigible, as unresponsive to treatment, as the psychological issues that individuals face.

Moreover, many will dispute that the cumulative public significances of these movements is positive. It can be argued that the proliferation of new networks and cultural practices is merely a further symptom of social malaise—a selfish retreat into personal, individual preoccupations, reflecting an abandonment of the aspiration to truly political values. It can also be pointed out that reactionary, fundamentalist, religious movements can be seen as attempting, in their own rather different terms, a form of resacralisation. But what gets highlighted when religious fundamentalism is brought into the picture is the vastness of the energy pool available for the political reforms that are urgently needed (see Chapter Eight).

Can therapists really make a difference?

Although enthusiastic about psychotherapy's role in participating in the refreshing of political culture, I am also somewhat sceptical. So my answer to this question "Can therapists really make a difference?" is both "No" and "Yes". Let's deal with "No" first, with the pessimism. James Hillman and Michael Ventura (1992) wrote a book called *We've Had a Hundred Years of Psychotherapy and the World's Getting Worse*. It is fairly clear what they were getting at—that psychotherapy makes little or no impact on an unjust world and that people in therapy are cut off from taking responsibility for ameliorating such injustice (they are cut off from their political energy by therapy that takes all available psychic energy for its own project of personal exploration). Yet I think that a much more accurate title for their book would have been *We've Had a Hundred Years of Psychotherapy Trying to Improve the World but the World's Stayed Pretty Much the Same*. For it is not a new project for psychotherapists to want to do something in relation to the world (see Foster, Moskowitz, & Javier, 1996; Totton, 2000). Freud wanted it, Jung wanted it, and the great pioneers of humanistic psychotherapy such as Maslow, Rogers, and Perls all wanted it as well. All of these people and their followers invited the world into therapy but the world didn't show up for its first therapy session. There are good reasons why the world didn't show up, not just resistance. One reason is that therapists so much want and need to be right! (Me too, this shadow issue of the analyst's maddening rectitude is not one I pretend to have fully dealt with). Therapists want to reduce everything to the special knowledge that they have. This kind of reductionism gets therapy a bad name when it comes to political and social issues. For example, I remember reading in the London *Guardian* an article—later the object of intense ridicule—by a Kleinian psychoanalyst about the phallic symbolism of cruise missiles going down ventilator shafts in Baghdad. My Jungian colleagues are just as bad when they tell us that the military-industrial complex is all the responsibility of the Greek God Hephaestus. The world won't listen to that level of explanation from psychotherapists and is right not to. The priority for psychotherapists is to embark on multidisciplinary work.

But there is more than therapy reductionism that has stopped us from being useful outside of a few specific areas such as psychoanalytically influenced social casework or, in some countries, child welfare legislation. Overall there is a fairly bad record to own up to. Psychotherapists of various kinds have colluded with oppressive regimes in Nazi Germany, the former Soviet Union, Argentina, and South Africa. They have been involved in dubious activities such as sending soldiers suffering from shellshock and battle fatigue back to the line of battle in both World Wars. In addition to that kind of bad record, there is also the ever-present collusion of psychotherapy with all manner of normative and oppressive practices at home, ranging from the psychopathological stigmatisation of lesbians and gay men (which still continues in many implicit ways in a wide range of locations (see Davies & Neal, 2000; Magee & Miller, 1997), or the easy joining in by therapists all over the world in right-wing politicians' attacks on father-lacking lone parent families usually headed by women. On this right-wing reading, these families, totally responsible for spoiling our wonderful world, only need a father or father figure to come back to sort them out. I love fathers and was one of the first to write about what good-enough fathers actually do, especially with their bodies, in furthering the sexual, aggressive, and spiritual development of their children (1986, 1989, 1993, 2001). But I utterly loathe the damaging idealisation of fathers that so many Western politicians have gone in for, backed by complacent analysts, therapists, and other mental health professionals (Later, in Chapter Nine, I will develop further these ideas about the father).

Then there is the problematic matter of psychotherapy's implicit claim that Western androcentric, middle-class values and ways of thinking hold and have value universally and are superior to and can be imposed on the values and ways of thinking of non-Western cultures (see Adams, 1996; Kareem & Littlewood, 1992; Luepnitz, 1988). Clearly, these unspoken assumptions reflect the typical caseloads of analysts and therapists, especially in private practice, in many countries (but see Altman, 1995). The treatment of women within much psychoanalytic thinking and practice has also been damaging to some. The rise of feminist and gender-sensitive psychotherapy has had an important impact in ameliorating this situation (e.g., Eichenbaum & Orbach, 1982). And what a lot of therapists and analysts say about men is also beginning to receive the same kind of critique that definitions of and generalisations about women used to receive.

Another reason why people are not so likely to listen to therapists who want to make a difference in the world is that therapists are completely crazy in their own professional politics, and the way they organise themselves radiates that craziness. No profession has been quite as subject to splits as the therapy profession, no profession has so frequently used personal demonisation and pathological pigeonholing to deal with and get rid of troublesome outsiders and those who question from within (Turkle, 1979).

Continuing to look at why we world-oriented therapists do not have a client, for reasons that I do not fully understand even now, the therapy world has tragically split its clinical project off from its sociocritical project. Frankfurt School writers and Lacanian theorists rarely talk of clients, or in an ordinary way about people: mothers, fathers, families, marriages, dreams, symptoms, sexuality, aggression, the inner world of the imagination. And when we read most clinical texts, the external world is hardly mentioned. Much therapy still seems (or claims) to take place in a political vacuum. There are several delusional aspects of this virginal fantasy about what we do. One delusion is that there are no politics going on the session itself, whereas many clinicians know how the power dynamics and imbalances of the typical therapy set-up cannot be wished away by reference to parental transference or the Law of the Father. These power imbalances often involve the denial of difference of any kind between therapist and client, the bending of the client to the moral will of the therapist, and the ongoing issue of sexual misconduct (Samuels, 1996).

Surveys of psychotherapists and counsellors show that they hear more from their clients about the political world than they used to. There are links between what is seen on the news and our emotional lives. But what does it mean when people use psychological language about a political or social issue? If you say you feel depressed or guilty about the environment, climate change, species depletion—what are you saying?

The way many psychotherapists understand depression is that it results from feeling angry and destructive towards someone you basically love and need. That is why bereaved people can become depressed. They may feel at some level that their bad feelings towards the dead person somehow caused the death. Or they may be angry at having been left. In either case, there is a feeling of being responsible that leads to guilt, self-reproach (often of delusional proportions), and very low spirits with a lack of emotional, cognitive, and physical energy.

It's that feeling of guilty responsibility that interests psychotherapists such as myself who want to bring therapy thinking to bear on political problems. In terms of climate change, for example, we can see similar dynamics (though it's important to be careful in mapping off from individual psychology to collective psychology). We love the earth yet we can see how destructive we can be towards it. Our guilt then paralyses us and we enter a political depression that we struggle to overcome. Hence it is not surprising that cutting-edge thinking in the therapy world considers that depression has social and political roots and does not only have to do with mums, dads, partners, sex, and all the usual therapy lines.

The question of anger comes up in relation to almost any political theme: economics, multiculturalism, war. It doesn't matter which side of a debate you are on, and you do not have to be directly affected to feel angry, though excluded and disadvantaged people are, of course, more likely to. The point is that when you have anger in a form that cannot be managed or resolved, you will find some kind of depression and guilt.

Leadership is the political theme that gets my clients the most worked up. In psychotherapy, we use the term "good-enough". This is taken from developmental theory where it is used in relation to a parent figure who is neither idealised as perfect nor denigrated in an angry way for having failed. Failure is, as parents know, inevitable. The question is whether children manage to tolerate their parents' failures. In politics, the place where we urgently need something like good-enough is in relation to our leaders. At present, we tend to build them up and idealise them so that they can have dictatorial powers even in a democratic society. Then, as we saw in the case of Tony Blair, the populace and the media work together to destroy the hitherto invulnerable leader (I return to the topic of the good-enough leader in the next chapter).

I'd like to suggest that the problem with our polity is not apathy. The problem is, rather, too much passion, too many aspirations, a belief in perfect solutions—leading, inevitably, to disappointment and withdrawal. What looks like apathy is actually a pervasive sense of powerlessness, often coupled with intensely guilty self-criticism. This is where the insights of psychotherapy might be useful. If we can accept that political perfection is unattainable, if we ask of ourselves only that we be good-enough citizens (just as we can only hope for good-enough leaders), we may be freed from the sense of depressive despair that mires us at present, so that political hope can reawaken.

The inner politician—an experiential approach

Now the chapter and its language become more experiential and personal in an attempt to conduct an exploration of what I call "the inner politician". At this point, I would like to invite readers to participate in the first of the experiential exercises that are scattered throughout the book. Although an unusual practice in a book of this kind, I have come to see that such exercises offer an emotional (as opposed to an intellectual) grounding for ideas that are intended to be of effective use in the world, and are not offered only as further evidence of the maddening rectitude of psychoanalysis. Readers can do the exercises alone or with someone else.

Where did you get your politics from? I think this is a question worth asking. What influence did your mother have on the politics you now have? Or your father? And what about differences in political outlook between your parents? Some people have been influenced in their political development by significant other people: teachers, priests, an older friend at school. Were you? The sex you are is really very significant in the kind of attitude to politics that you will have. Your sexual orientation is equally important. Lesbians and gay men live more closely to those political aspects and nuances of life than straight people do. Class and socio-economic factors are obviously central, too, and so is one's ethnic, religious, and national background.

There is a common experience in Western societies of feeling oppressed by a domestic tyrant, whether male or female, or seeing other family members as oppressed, that can give rise to a sharp sense of injustice and embryonic revolutionary feelings.

Sometimes, when I talk to people about what has formed their politics they start to speak about an event or moment in history that they can remember—their first political memory, meaning the first time they became aware that there is a political system with power at its core, including disparities of wealth and influence.

If some readers are following along in this experiential political journey, then ask yourselves "What are my first political memories?"

Another way to look at the notion of the inner politician is to imagine a political energy scale, where ten stands for political fanaticism, even martyrdom. Zero stands for absolute passivity and a total lack of interest in politics.

Where would you place yourself right now in your life, what level of political energy do you have?

Then you can play around with the scale. When you're with people of the same sex does the energy level go up or down or stay the same? Is it higher at home or at work? Are there some issues that send it skyrocketing and some issues that bring it down? Think of the last big interpersonal disagreement or fight with someone you love. Could it be that there was a different level of political energy at work in each of you?

Let's take this thinking right into the traditional heartland of psychotherapy.

What was your mother's level of political energy compared to yours, or to your father's? More widely, what was your level compared to the typical level of the street or neighbourhood in which you grew up?

Continuing to sketch the inner politician, I come to the question of "political style". I have noticed in the conflict resolution work that I have done that the various people in conflict are often operating not only with very different levels of political energy but also in very different political styles.

Hence, in my work as a political consultant, I am using the idea of conflicting political styles in many settings. The inspiration in overall terms was Jung's model of psychological types: extroversion, introversion, thinking, feeling, sensation, intuition. As in life generally, for a variety of reasons, some of them to do with their personal backgrounds, some to do with their inborn political constitutions, people will live out the political aspects of themselves in different ways. Some will be violent terrorists; some pacifists. Some will want empirical backup for their ideas; others will fly by the seat of their pants. Some will definitely enjoy co-operative political activity; others will suffer the nightmare of trying to accomplish things in a group only because they passionately believe in the ends being pursued. As we begin to make a start on working out a psychologically driven transformative politics, let us not make the mistake of insisting that everyone do it in precisely the same way. If we are to promote political creativity, we need to value and honour diverse political styles and types, and to think of ways of protecting such diversity (I return to the question of political style and type in Chapter Five).

For now, let me just record that the notion of political style is useful when addressing conflict, whether interpersonal or within organisations or even between nations or parts of nations. Just as introverts and extroverts suffer from mutual incomprehension, people or groups that employ a particular political style often have very little idea about how the other person or group is actually "doing" their politics. This is not to say that political content per se is irrelevant, only that there may be more that divides opponents than their different views.

Politics and psychotherapy

Attempts are constantly made to improve things in the political world, usually by redistributing wealth or changing legislative and constitutional structures or defusing warlike situations. It is not that nothing is being tried to make things better. Equally vigorous attempts are made to resist and contest such changes and most social systems have a gigantic impersonal capacity to resist change anyway. But projects of reform are valuable and necessary and will generate their own psychological changes. For example, the consequences of fair and effective minimum wage legislation or devolving power to the regions of a country or amending the constitution would have effects that would show up on any "national emotional audit".

But a materialist approach deriving exclusively from economics, or one that depends solely on altering the structures of the state, will not refresh those parts of the individual citizen that a psychological perspective can reach. Our disappointment at liberal democracy's failure to deliver the spiritual goods and our growing realisation that there are limits to what can be achieved by economic redistribution or altering constitutional structures, strengthen my overall argument: something is missing in contemporary Western politics that involves a calamitous denial of the secret life at its core. We can change the clothes, shift the pieces around, but the spectre that haunts materialist and constitutional moves in the political world is that they only ruffle the surface. They do not (because, alone, they cannot) bring about the transformations for which the political soul yearns.

Nevertheless, the perspectives advocated here may never, ever, be applied to our political culture. Everything psychotherapists and analysts have said or done may fail to make one iota of difference to the condition of the world. I am a sceptic. But I am also an enthusiast and the next chapter contains examples of that enthusiasm in relation to key political problems such as aggression and leadership.

CHAPTER TWO

Aggression and leadership

In the first chapter, I tried to set out what I think is possible and what is not possible for psychotherapists when it comes to the application of our ideas and practices to the world of politics. People writing from a therapy perspective need to be careful not to come over just as intelligent journalists or commentators on politics, or as bloggers. What would be the point of that? But we also do not want to descend into psychobabble or use abstract technical language that could never be operationalised.

As I mentioned in the previous chapter, over the past fifteen years I have built an international practice as a political consultant working with leading politicians in Britain and the US, and with advisers, parties, and activist groups in several countries—so what I will say is grounded in experience. In particular, I seem to have gravitated to work in the general area of nationalism, national identity, and nation building (in South Africa, Brazil, Poland, and Russia) and this informs what I write (see also Samuels, 2001, pp. 186–194).

Imagine—politics!

Let us talk about the state we are in: despite occasional moments of hope, it is primarily a state of agony, the agony of political rupture. A profound cultural depression and demoralisation has seized the West. Power-hungry elites flourish in most Western countries, as well as elsewhere.

As I suggested in the previous chapter, depression on the cultural scale resembles depression on the personal level. Just as in personal depression, politically we also see paralysis of thought and action in one part of the system, together with buried but very high levels of self-reproach and guilt in another part.

The key feature of depression, personally and politically, is being unable to manage aggression. Many therapists agree that fantasies of destruction of the other, who is also much loved and needed, leads to a profound sense and fear of loss, and hence to mourning. Guilt and self-reproach follow. If you do not manage your aggression, then you will get depressed. But my point about depression and aggression is a more global one, given the way many nations shoot first and ask questions afterwards. (See Samuels, 1989, pp. 194–215 for a discussion of cultural depression during the Cold War.) When a country possesses apocalyptic power, it is most certainly at risk of depression. It is not easy for the US, or the West, to live with its awesome destructive power; our very strength and success lead to our cultural depression. Global one-sidedness is also a psychological problem for the victorious.

There is indeed a kind of political agony abroad. The body bears this agony just as much as mind and psyche (the word *agon* means to writhe). How do we understand the current Western epidemic of (or at least anxiety over) obesity except as a sign of agony? Or agony via environmentally created diseases. The bodies of the citizens are always armoured against attack or loss, there is no clean political air for people to breathe, and a constant state of political adrenalisation. We can take the suffering body as politically diagnostic.

Could we imagine there ever being a therapy for politics? To do so, we would want to foreground the connections between social change and personal change (as detailed by several authors in Layton, Hollander, & Gutwill, 2006). I am asking for an imagining of a politics that is dreamy, subversive, out-of-order, disputing what is said to be realistic and what is said to be hopelessly idealistic. If anyone points out that some idea or other is not realistic, in such a politics, we tell them to look at what the realistic people have done to us. Ideals and visions are the only things that can undermine a toxic social order, coming in on the side of the oppressed.

Experiential exercise (for two people)

This is about political emotions as carried by the citizen's (reader's) body. Such emotions are likely to be mixed, ranging, as I suggested earlier, from hope to disappointment at the state of national or global politics.

> This exercise is ideally done in pairs but individual readers can try it in front of a mirror. What the two (or more) of you have to do is to stand up, face your fellow participant(s), make eye contact, sculpt your political pain by using your whole body to adopt a pose or a series of movements (or any physical expression that comes spontaneously). Share this with your partner(s) by showing them what has come up and try to take in what they have come up with, then relax and reflect for a few moments. Then, do this again, probably repeating the sculpt but this time adding a sound or sounds, not so much words as an expressive vocalisation. Watch as before, and also listen to what is happening in the room as these sounds come out and intermingle. When you are done, take a moment to share your feelings and reactions with your partner, or write them down if you are doing it on your own.

Good-enough leadership

Political theory and practice has assumed there are two main approaches to leadership. There is hierarchical and heroic leadership based on male authority and a masculine approach to knowledge that assumes there is one objectively true social story. In this model, there are good leaders and there are bad leaders and we all have our lists of them. Weber (1924) had this kind of leader in mind when he referred to the "charismatic leader". This kind of leader is often seen these days as a problem (see O'Connor, Mumford, Clifton, Gessner, & Connelly, 1995).

A second approach is much more collaborative, involving a kind of metaphorical sibling model of leadership. But although appealing and sometimes usable, sibling leadership is just too demanding on citizens to be in operation all the time. People duck-dive for cover; they do not necessarily mean to become bystanders but they do not see any other way to manage the burden of being collaborative leaders.

So there is heroic leadership and there is collaborative leadership. For many years, I have been advocating for a third kind of leader—the good-enough leader. It is an idea taken from therapy thinking about the family. Donald Winnicott (1971) said that parents and babies have to find a middle way between the baby's idealisation and denigration of the parent. There is a natural tendency of a baby to idealise her parent but when things go in a less than perfect way (as they surely will), it flips over into denigration.

Sound familiar? An initial idealisation, then a failure to deliver things perfectly, then denigration? It is meant to sound familiar. The media depends on it. Because this is how we respond to leaders, first by passively following the idealised leader, then seeking out feet of clay. What can we do about the pattern?

We must try to change how we position "success" and "failure". I know the word "failure" hurts people's feelings because it is so in-your-face. Failure means falling short, being imperfect, fallible, only passable, fucking up—an all too human lack of potency. Yet maybe what we need nowadays are "can't do" politicians, impotent politicians—they are that, anyway, are they not?—as the financial crisis of late 2008 showed us.

Maybe being only "in control" is not always valuable. Winnicott wrote that "we succeed by failing—failing the patient's way" (1963, p. 258). I would add that failure by a leader paves the way for greater contributions and more autonomy on the part of citizens. The leader fails the citizens but in the citizens' own way.

Bob Dylan nibbled away at the success-failure binary when he sang "There's no success like failure and failure's no success at all". And on 9 September 2007 Bill Clinton was reported on CNN as speaking of the inevitability of failure in politics in relation to his health care plan. I believe it was the first time he had explicitly spoken in that vein. When Harold Macmillan, the British Prime Minister, was asked by a journalist in 1963 what had brought him down, he replied "Events, dear boy, events".

Yet Rumi wrote in his poem "Desire and the importance of failing" (2006) that "failure is the key to the kingdom". Good-enoughness always involves failure. The key thing is how to manage failure, even to see failure as an art. Samuel Beckett wrote (1983) that we have to "fail better". Disappointment is difficult, for sure, but it, too, has to be managed.

So the good-enough leader can accept the likelihood of failure, in a post-heroic take on leadership. But there is a head-heart problem here and it is a cultural complex as defined by Singer and Kimbles (2004). In our heads, we often know that the old-style leaders are dangerous, but in our hearts and guts we feel we need the fatherly protection they offer. In our souls, we are in love with the heroic leader whose Führer-eroticism turns us on. In our heads, we agree with Brecht's Galileo (1947): "Unhappy is the land that has need of heroes." Could we become more aware of our abusive love affair with heroic leaders?

There is a definite gender issue here. Some of the collective responses over the years to Hillary Clinton show how hard it is for a female leader to fulfil compellingly the role of a heroic leader. On the one hand, this is a welcome development because, as I have been suggesting, we often enter into abusive relationships with such leaders. On the other hand, there is a kind of literalism and essentialism in play in which a woman can never fulfil any of the functions we associate to "father". So what female leaders have to do is to be deadlier than the male, as we saw in Britain with Mrs Thatcher. The great thing about good-enough leaders is that they can be good-enough leaders of whatever sex.

So far so good (-enough). But what happens to our good-enough leaders when things get violent. This is where good-enough leadership appears to hit a rock. What happens when things get warlike? Where does good-enough leadership leave us with respect to violent action? This question will not go away, whether we are talking about legitimate war, illegitimate war, state terror and violently repressive action, or suicide bombing and the cult of the martyr.

Do we not need masculine virtues then? In a time of "terror" and war without end, are not the conservatives right? Do we not need paternal security and a national father's protection then? The hell with nurture! Let us see about that, as I turn now to some discussion of fathers and of men. As stated, I am preparing the ground for suggestions about new ways to think, imagine, and manage conflict.

New ideas about fathers and conflict

Let us consider the question: Are men powerful? In a way, they are. They own things, they control women and children, they earn more for the same work, they can fight and protect others. But is this the whole picture?

Psychoanalysis is fond of pointing out male fear of the mother, of the feminine, the abject swamp which they must never slip into. Male power is seen as a reaction to and a denial of this fear. This is not wrong, but there is more to say. There are several vulnerable groups of men: men of colour, gay men, ill men, prisoners, soldiers, physically challenged, poor men, unemployed men. We need to hold this in a balance with obvious male power.

It is worth asking what would happen if men used their power to help others with less power? What if more men as a group spoke out as men against the bonus culture, in favour of a fairer distribution of wealth, against the use of military action? How could such a scene-shifting speak-out happen? What can we do? What do we need?

First we need a positive account of the father that does not stupidly build him up to an unrealistic degree. An account that makes it much more difficult for our old-style political leaders to masquerade as the only kind of fathers that there could be. An account that does not dwell on the malevolent power of the father's body but on its affirming physical warmth, a warmth as much aggressive as erotic. Not on his holding the mother who holds the children but on his holding of the children himself. The stay-at-home father, the sensitive and affirming father, the playful father, the wounded and unhappy father, not the punitive, stern self-contained father. Not the commander-in-chief father. We need a story of the father in which emotional security is as important as physical security. That would be a useful beginning to an equally new and analogous story about political leadership.

Not all paternal aggression is harmful, though, and there is a role for fathers in transforming the aggression of their children from mindless violence into healthy roaring self-assertion.

If there is no father present, and when lone parents are women, there may be very unexpected outcomes. Lone mothers can understand what fathers do that is good and useful, and we know that they work out ways of doing that themselves. Maybe not in the same way but they can do it. Even when it comes to questions of discipline and authority, lone mothers can do it—there is a secret hardness to the female body (See Samuels, 2001, pp. 101–121 for further discussion of issues concerning lone parents—and see Chapter Nine).

Now let us take these ideas about men and fathers and play them back into the political arena and what I was saying about how hard it is to escape the abusive relationship with the heroic leader. If we change what we think about men and fathers, alter what we expect of them, engage with these questions—then perhaps what we think about leaders, what we expect of them, can change as well .

But there will still be this nagging doubt. What if there is real, actual political conflict and violence, war, terror? Will we not need the martial values then? Someone is bound to remind us that Winston Churchill said that "courage is ... the first of human qualities because it ... guarantees all others". My nuanced and openly ambivalent answer is "Yes and no". It all depends on how we approach the question of conflict.

Aggressive conflict is an idea that must be addressed by analysts and therapists as much as by political thinkers and politicians. It is very hard to think about aggressive conflict because the topic is so frightening. How can we evaluate aggression objectively, deciding what is mindless destructiveness and what is justifiable self-assertion? Who says when a war is just and when it is not? Can aggression ever be managed and to what degree? Is aggression biologically primary in humans or secondary, something social and psychological, the result of frustration and alienation? Psychoanalysis has worked the aggressive field since its beginnings. More recently, new thinking has brought out the hidden relational virtues of aggression. These include getting in touch with the other, and there is a small literature on aggression as a mode of relating that allows for self-interest and self-assertion (e.g., Searles, 1973, p. 325; Storr, 1970, p. 57).

From the perspective of the political psyche, I think we need to seriously revalue the presence of aggression in the pursuit of social justice. My study of South African politics suggests that without the forceful military contributions of Umkhonto we Sizwe (Spear of the Nation, the military wing of the African National Congress), plus the South African Communist Party, and the mainly Black Cuban troops in Angola, we would not have seen the new South Africa. No Mandela, no Truth and Reconciliation Commission, no books on restorative justice. And, to complicate it even more, all of these were financed and supported by the Soviet Union.

From the point of view of gender psychology, aggression, and especially aggressive fantasy, can be an individuation path, especially for women: an imaginary way to be thrusting, penetrative, and seminal, to break out of the coils of Eros where the woman is only responsive to the needs of others in a reproduction of mothering. From the point of view of moral philosophy, there is a critical *telos* for aggression. How can you develop concern for an other if there is no reason to do so? Aggression is required to be present for concern (and the depressive position) to flower. From the point of view of metapsychology, aggression is part of ego-consciousness—the way we strive to become conscious by breaking wholes into parts. The very etymology of "analysis" is aggressive— Erich Neumann said that symbols of consciousness involved the teeth and biting (1954, p. 124).

We know how relative a matter aggression is. You see this in terms of gender all the time. But are women really less aggressive than men? We can also see an immense cultural and ethical relativism with regard to political aggression. I will give a complicated and controversial example. As one who has been deeply immersed in the politics of the Middle East, I have been struck by the way the interrelation of Jews and aggression seems very problematic for all parties. We can note this as originating in Western and Arab responses to the birth of modern Zionism and the establishment of the pre-World War Two settler communities in Palestine, through intense soul-searching about the Holocaust. For example, we have seen debates on alleged Jewish "passivity" on the one hand and the valorous resistance of the Warsaw Ghetto on the other hand. And then the discussion will move on to the aggressive policies of the State of Israel. Whatever one's position on Israel/Palestine, it is possible to agree, I think, that thoughtful discussion is interfered with by ethnically based assumptions and generalisations about aggression.

These reflections on aggression have been stimulated and complexified by my participation in much interfaith dialogue work recently. I believe there is a faith background to much of the aggressive conflict we see in the Middle East. In these dialogue groups, composed of Jews, Christians, and Muslims, the Jews who were present, including myself, learned from the Imams about the Islamic idea of ta'aruf found in 49:13 of the Qur'an: "Oh Humanity, we have created of you male and female, and have made you peoples and tribes, that you might come to know one another."

I find this a brilliantly inspiring take on difference and the aggressive conflict that an encounter with difference brings. It is not at all like the Tower of Babel. In this reading of things, a point or purpose (telos) is given to difference. If we want to know an other, that other has to be different from ourselves. But that brings in the question of aggressive conflict and even violence.

There is more to this than knowing the other, important though that is. Full engagement and dialogue with an other benefits the self. As this Qur'anic principle of ta'aruf has it, all kinds of differences—gender, national, religious—have the hidden potential to enable people to get to know themselves better and more deeply. Here we find a fascinating congruence between Islamic social thought and psychoanalytic ideas about the interconnectedness of hate and love and how an aggressive act may also reflect a great desire for contact and touch.

Both Islam and psychoanalysis understand that conflict and aggression will arise, whether we like it or not. But conflict and aggression are also part of relationality and recognition, that is what I am saying. So it matters what our attitude to aggressive conflict is. Far from being abstract and of little political relevance, this is the key political issue of our times. Each nation is, as it were, inhabited by the existence of other nations. But other nations present a threat that cannot be cancelled out by visions of global love.

The note on which I want to conclude this section of the chapter is a few lines from Wilfred Owen's Great War poem "The Parable of the Old Man and the Young" (1916), which offers a completely different ending to the story of Abraham and Isaac that we could take as a profound warning of a terrible future. We pick up the narrative at the point the Angel of the Lord appears:

> When lo! an Angel called him out of heaven,
> Saying, Lay not they hand upon the lad,
> Neither do anything to him, thy son.
> Behold! Caught in a thicket by its horns
> A Ram. Offer the Ram of Pride instead.
> But the old man would not so, but slew his son,
> And half the seed of Europe, one by one.

Getting out of the American box

Think about aggression, and the role and history of the United States cannot be avoided. Every year the American historian William Blum publishes his "updated summary of the record of US foreign policy". This shows that, since 1945, the US has tried to overthrow more than fifty governments, many of them democratically elected; grossly interfered in elections in thirty countries; bombed the civilian populations of thirty countries; used chemical and biological weapons; and attempted to assassinate foreign leaders.

In many cases Britain has been a collaborator. The degree of human suffering, let alone criminality, is little acknowledged in the West, despite the presence of the world's most advanced communications and nominally most free journalism. That the most numerous victims of terrorism—"our" own terrorism—are Muslims, is unsayable. That extreme jihadism, which led to 9/11, was nurtured as a weapon of Anglo-American policy (Operation Cyclone in Afghanistan) is suppressed.

It is reasonable to ask why and how this has been happening, why and how we tolerate it, particularly we who are not Americans but closely connected to and allied with Americans. Therefore, I want to think in terms of denationalising the psyche, stopping the pattern in which individuals are educated to think like states. We need to reimage ourselves, not as citizens of one country, and not as citizens of the world (which is such a cliché), but more as nomads, bums, travelling folk, itinerants, of no fixed abode, homeless, drifters.

Why? To see if we can get outside of our national box or world-view, to go beyond what is best for Americans or Brits, getting out of our places to put ourselves in the places of others, part of a quest for a more empathic connection with other countries and groups. This could actually be economically effective, a sort of win-win approach to international relations. Or, to be more dignified, part of a truly ethical approach to foreign policy in which, following Levinas, we love the other "because he is yourself", or, following Rozensweig, we call "speaking listening", or, adapting Buber, relate "we" to "we" (see Seidler, 2007 for a fuller account).

On occasion, I have asked American audiences to imagine a world that did not have America in it, so that taking an American viewpoint becomes much more difficult. Then to think of something like 9/11. How hard it is to give up the idea that something had to be done, by something like the United Nations if not by the US itself. How maddening and infuriating it must have been for many Americans, maybe the majority, to find that some people with other national backgrounds did not respond to the towers tumbling down in an American way.

I trust it is clear that I am not asking American readers to imagine themselves as not existing. This is not my sadism, and the response I seek is not the reader's masochism. I am trying to create a moment's space for an experiment in political thinking. If you can get out of the American box with respect to 9/11, then it is surely possible with respect to many other less terrible though no less important issues and images. Outside the American box, ask yourself about the possibility of not responding or retaliating militarily to 9/11 at all. Doing nothing.

Let me paint the picture in a little more detail. As Christianity has it, could the US have "turned the other cheek"? After all, in the Book of Proverbs it says: "If thine enemy be hungry, give him bread to eat. And if he be thirsty give him water to drink. Say not, I will do to him as he hath done to me." Psychoanalysts and psychotherapists place non-retaliation at the heart of their ethical and technical commitments to their patients, so many of them know about the huge power of non-retaliation—and we know that retaliation usually fixes nothing.

Please know that I am not saying what America (or the West) should or should not have done, just trying to establish some parameters for a different kind of discussion about it.

Outside the American or Western box, we see that the world lives and suffers under conditions of profound cultural inequality. I mean more than international finance and trade, weapons and war, or control of the media. Cultural inequality is a qualitative thing not a quantitative thing: it is a total and all pervasive condition, it is not part of the field of international relations—it is the field. The most egregious present-day cultural inequality exists between the West and the Islamic world.

It is interesting to recall Jung's (1963) dream before he visited the Arab countries of North Africa. How he had to struggle with an Arab prince (really fight with him) before each could hear the other's point of view—and for Jung to feel that the prince would understand him. The dream, said Jung, corrected (compensated) his initial wrong attitude that he was somehow above or superior to the people he was going to visit.

More important than Jung, even, is Genesis 21. After Sarah caused Abraham to expel Hagar the Egyptian handmaiden, with her young son Ishmael, for mocking her, it seems as if Ishmael and Hagar will die. "Hagar lifted up her voice and wept. The Angel of God said: 'What aileth thee, Hagar? Fear not, for God hath heard the voice of the lad where he is … Arise, lift up the lad and hold him in thy hand: for I will make him a great nation.'"

But we have this different world of profound cultural inequality: a psychological and spiritual malaise, not only a political one. An unequal world will always be an unsafe world. A safer world needs to be a more equal world.

Political transformation and personal responsibility

I hope we can at least imagine a utopic move out of the social and political conditions in which we find ourselves. For if we cannot, then there will be no personal growth, change, transformation—no therapy or analysis, really. It means that every single client in *personal* distress has to have, or to work on, a little bit of a utopic *social* vision.

If we are going to transform politics, we will have to take full responsibility for the act. We may need less mature reflection and more impulsive and passionate action, more doing and less being. More organising and more struggle—sometimes, more fighting. Do not just sit there ... And if not now, when?

What about hope? There can be none if idealism is rejected out of hand. I condemn so-called "realistic" people; I cannot stand them. Maybe I should not condemn, merely note that their realism is just a special version of idealism, their well-trained lack of sentiment a secret romanticism, their nihilism just as personally stabilising as any political ideology.

All of this brings us back to the whole question of good-enoughness—now in the form of the good-enough citizen, a political subject who can accept his or her own failures. This is so important because anticipated shame at failure, as opposed to a readiness to work with such a feeling, is what destroys the impulse and the capacity for action.

But if we can accept that political perfection is unattainable, if we ask of ourselves only that we be good-enough citizens (just as we can only hope for good-enough leaders), we may be freed from the underlying sense of despair that paralyses us at present, so that our political hopes and impulses can truly bear fruit.

We need to imagine a better politics because it is almost impossible to imagine a worse. On that journey, we will have to own infatuation with heroic leaders, and try to end the abusive relationship we have with them by making it possible for good-enough leaders to come on stream. These new figures will have quite different attitudes to what their role as national "fathers" or parents might be.

The move from economic sadism to relational economics that I write about in the next chapter can directly affect the level of aggressive political conflict in our societies and in the world. Then the Islamic idea of *ta'aruf* may teach us fresh ways to manage such conflict. Diversity has been visited upon us for benevolent reasons: sure, diversity often leads to conflict—but conflict often masks the deepest desire to get in touch and communicate.

No transformation or resacralisation of politics will happen outside of the field of personal responsibility. But we have to exercise such responsibility from inside the cesspit, not from outside it. We need to be forgiving towards ourselves, as we will fail to honour commitments and fail to deliver on promises. Above all, we cannot and should not seek to be more than good-enough citizens. But anyone and everyone can reimagine the world. We are each one of us co-creators, destroyers, and saviours of the world we live in. We should begin our work now, here, among one another, and also in solitude (I return to the question of personal responsibility for things political in Chapter Five).

I will conclude these reflections on personal responsibility with a highly salient untitled holocaust poem written in Polish by Jerzy Ficowski and translated by Keith Bosley (1979):

> I did not manage to save
> a single life
>
> I did not know how to stop
> a single bullet
>
> And I wander round cemeteries
> which are not there
>
> I look for words
> which are not there
> I run
>
> to help where no one called
> to rescue after the event
>
> I want to be on time
> even if I am too late

CHAPTER THREE

The economic psyche

Psychotherapy and economics

In the opening two chapters, we saw that the hallowed project of linking psychotherapy and the world is not a new one (Totton, 2000). We saw that all too often the world does not show up for its first session. This is sad and wasteful because more therapists than ever before want to realise the social and political potential of our profession. Yet there still remains a huge gap between what we wish and what is the case, between wanting to play a role in social and political life and getting results. Nowhere is this gap more apparent than in relation to economics.

My interest in economics led to my working with Britain's Financial Services Authority (the then statutory regulator of the personal finance industry) to elaborate the psychological difficulties facing its agenda concerning "fairness" with regard to personal financial products. Although fairness is stated on their website to be the core value of the industry, there was also an admission that it is not easy to say what fairness really is when it comes to personal finance!

Anyone, not just a therapist, who seeks to improve anything in the social realm is up against massive, impersonal forces that do not want change: the economic system, patriarchy, the world's warlords. But there is a further paradoxical problem. The human unconscious and the human soul are the sources of imagination, creativity, and hope. Yet, to a degree, they are also the sources of our problems. In its cruel, negative, and sadistic aspects, the unconscious is indeed, as Freud taught, conservative (Freud, 1933). It resists improvement and transformation as well as promoting them. The very thing that gives us hope that solutions might be found is also the source of the problems that cry out for solutions.

Prior to a conference at which I was due to talk about the economy, a friend said "Nobody will dispute that economics is important, but everyone will offer different reasons why." That was true. In this chapter, I am weaving in and out of the present economic crisis and I truly do not want to speak just like any intelligent journalist about austerity and the recession. I want to stick to the language of psychotherapy.

Like many, I am fascinated by and in support of many new ideas about economics, ideas about fresh approaches to taxation, or a "new bottom line", or a more "family friendly" approach to economics, or concerning the emotional cost of debt and anxiety about losing money in the crisis, or sustainable economics, or ending global economic inequality. I have written and spoken about these things and about the abject failure of market capitalism to meet people's emotional and spiritual needs since the late 1980s when I joined forces with the New Economics Foundation in Britain.

In this chapter, I am engaged in pursuing the tragic vision (Ricoeur, 1967) of psychoanalysis, asking: "If we want all these wonderful aspiring things in our economic lives, why haven't we got them already?" Is there a psychological deal breaker or delimiter we need to know more about?

Yet I do think it is possible, even within an impoverished political culture, to extend the vocabulary of economics. If we use the metaphor of an iceberg, where six-sevenths is below the surface, then we can say that most conventional economic analysis inhabits only the top seventh. We can begin to think beyond "exchange value" (cost or price) to consider "emotional value", "aesthetic value", and "sustainable value". So the emotional value of the environment or conservation area may be greater than that of the road or the supermarket. The development would also sacrifice aesthetic value. And if trees and natural habitats are destroyed, there's a cost in terms of sustainable value.

Why is economics important, then? Here are a few reasons why I think economics is important. The first reason, gloriously naive for sure, is an ethical one. Because of economic thinking and economic practices, people are suffering and dying every day. Anyone with a conscience has to try to evaluate what is going on in the economic sphere. Economics is the filter or culvert through which the vicissitudes of power, in all their complexity and cruelty, are passed. Where economics goes, violent conflict often follows.

Second, as we are witnessing daily, economics is extraordinarily influential on all of us. Paul Samuelson, Nobel laureate and writer of the most widely used basic text on economics, said: "Let those who will wrote the nation's laws, just so long as I can write its economic textbooks." In the 1930s, John Maynard Keynes made the claim that "Practical men, who believe themselves quite exempt from any intellectual influences, are usually the slaves of some defunct economist" (1936, p. 383).

What we find in today's economic discourses is an incredibly rapid re-evaluation of what is considered hopelessly idealistic and utopian and what is considered realistic and effective. It is not so long since the aspiration to live sustainable lives was considered irredeemably adolescent. Only a few anti-colonial lefties or nationalistic former freedom fighters used to care about redistribution of wealth between North and South. And the present preoccupation with climate change and environmental despoliation was, until pretty recently, the preserve of the sensitive amongst us or a few mad scientists.

We are in the midst of a huge shift in values and in collective consciousness—a profound, complex, nearly unbearable, perhaps doomed to fail psychological shift in our philosophies of life, with powerful implications for society and soul alike. Yet amidst this very shift we see dramatic and unmistakable evidence of retrogressive tendencies. The growth of inequality in countries such as the United States and Britain in the past thirty years has been repeatedly charted. So, too, has the damaging effect of inequality, whether in terms of fomenting violent social and international conflict, or in terms of literally creating ill-health (both physical and mental), or in the production of middle-class guilt, which is one of the main things that links analysts and their clients. Excessive disparities of wealth correlate internationally with levels of illness and mortality. It is better from the point of view of a good life to live in a poorer but less economically polarised country than in a much richer one that is very polarised (Pickett & Wilkinson, 2009).

Thinking about inequality for a moment, it is clear that a relationship exists between class and the individual's inner world. Many people have achieved a higher socio-economic status than their parents. And yet, in their inner worlds, encountered in therapy, in dreams perhaps, the social class they grew up in is still the social class they are in in terms of psychic reality and narrative truth. My first ever banker client dreamed of his father's coal mine all the time. The (male) solidarity of the miners—for example, when there was a disaster underground—struck him as different from the atmosphere and ethos of a large Wall Street investment bank. We did of course play a little with what we were "mining" in the analysis but the main thrust of our dialogue about these dreams was in terms of a thorough, many-layered, compassionate, and healing comparison of his entire situation with that of his father's. Not competition with the father. There's more to intergenerational male relating than Oedipus, and the work with this man reminded me of that. I'll return later to the benevolence of comparison compared to the malevolence of competition.

The typical move—or at least it used to be typical, the pattern is changing—is from working class to middle class. To the extent that a passion for social and economic justice exists (for good reasons) in the working class, you can see how destabilising and ego-dystonic their ruthless rise to the top is for some people. I have had a lot of clients like that. This point about class and the inner world applies with particular force when the patient is a member of a minority ethnic community. What can't be avoided is that we may be up against a psychodynamic barrier to social mobility. The good news is that I think that, clinically and culturally, we can do something about it.

That concludes my introduction to the chapter, which was intended to sensitise readers to the marriage of psychotherapy and economics. In the next section, I'm going to explore how we might move from what I call economic sadism to relational economics. Then I declare that "it's the psychology, stupid!" and, using a frankly experiential approach, take us on an economic night sea journey from an inferno of sadism to a relational utopia and back again. After that, there's a section on gender and economics because I think a psychotherapeutic perspective can be valuable there and it usually gets a fiery discussion going. And finally, issues of heart, soul, and spirit.

From economic sadism to relational economics

Like everyone, I have my own passionate views about all aspects of economics, ranging from doubts about the viability and fairness of the principle of wealth inheritance, to questioning usury and the practice of charging interest, to the perception that market economics works a bit like victor's justice—if you're making it, you're liking it. If you're in rural Africa or much of Europe today, you probably aren't liking it very much.

Differing economic systems reflect different ideas about human nature. Altruism versus self-interest, co-operation versus the survival of the fittest. But responses to the financial crisis made me realise that we do not have much of a handle on how people really experience economic life intrapsychically. In the economic psyche, images of wealth, poverty, and money have become numinous. We are captivated whether we want to be or not.

Since the invention of the joint stock company in the early seventeenth century (the Virginia Company being one of the first), and its refinement in the Scotland and France of the eighteenth century, there has been a growing invisibility of money, culminating in today's world of electronic transfer, credit cards, derivatives, and swaps. What does it mean for the psyche that there's this lack of actual lucre, filthy or otherwise, and the undoing of money qua money—notes, coins, cheques? The way the money and commodity markets work has reminded many of the way the unconscious works—unpredictable, contradictory, paradoxical, outside of conscious (read government) control. Just as we have never seen libido, as opposed to inferring it from experience, so, too, does money increasingly present us with the same problematic. And this is not only a developed world crisis, because are these not the very factors—global transfers of funds and so forth—that have made death-dealing and cruel international economic inequalities so easy to build and perpetuate?

As a thought experiment, I've been trying to imagine a society in which all income is earned income or stems from pensions and social security. There is little or no private ownership of capital. Estate taxes are very high. Inequalities of wealth are consensually regulated. Markets are tempered by collective commitment to collective well-being. When I first wrote this fantasy down, I noted in the margin: not such a madly utopic utopia, really.

> Please join me in imagining such an economy.

The thought experiment begs the questions of whether and how inequality would enter into the picture to the degree that we see it in today's

Western societies. For some people, the hypothesis would be that there is an ineluctable psychological basis to inequality and that humans would find a way to create social stratifications and even classes. Class being somehow an "archetypal" addiction. Or a Darwinian one. They would point to British schools in which all the students have to wear the same clothes as determined by the school ("uniforms" as we call them)—and yet myriad inequalities even in the sartorial realm cannot be excluded.

For others, the hypothesis would be that such changes in socio-economic organisation would lead to a celebration of difference that did not valorise inequality. We might reward success to a degree but we would not necessarily punish failure. In fact, it would be claimed, we should begin to dispute and heal the success-failure binary that afflicts everyone.

In contemporary psychotherapy, especially relational psychotherapy, you might say we seek to create something akin to a microcosmic version of the fantasy I began with in which injustice and inequality is reduced as far as is possible. We aspire to mutual recognition, in Jessica Benjamin's phrase (Benjamin, 1988), or to a joint immersion in the alchemical vessel if you want it in Jung's language. "The analyst is in the treatment as much as the patient", was his slogan.

Our critics say we are trying to flow uphill because inequality is the only quality that there is. We are trying to be too democratic, too equal, and, in our search for relational justice and recognition, in our denial of ineluctable inequality, we deludedly deprive the patient (not the client in this perspective) of what he or she really needs from therapy.

Holding the lines of the debate on equality and inequality in mind, what follows is an exploration of how the inner world works when it comes to economics. It is, as I said earlier, experiential, and I would ask the reader respectfully and sincerely to help me by trying to conjure up stuff from your own personal past history and present situation in order to engage with the questions I am asking. The present-day dynamics of the economic psyche are heavily inflected by money memories from the past.

It's the psychology, stupid!

For many years, in workshops on the theme of "The economic psyche", I have been exploring the interface of psychology and money. Part of the work is to consider the implications if people really were to take themselves, consciously, as society seems to take them—merely as economic agents, pursuing money and all that goes with that. What I am doing in the workshops is prescribing the symptom, in the language of family therapy. Look—you live in a society that valorises money and material things, right? Okay, what happens if you go with that, rather than protesting weakly about it? Can you undo the bondage to money and status by overdoing it?

At an economic psyche workshop in Pittsburgh about ten years ago, I asked the participants to introduce themselves purely as economic agents and then share with the others how that felt. They were being asked by me to stand up and say "I'm Andrew, I work as an X, I earn Y, I have Z amount of liabilities. My financial and economic goals are A, B, C." And other similar pieces of information were asked for. Buzz of anxious excitement in the room. Then a man gets to his feet—and, I recall later, he is the only one wearing a suit—and says "I'm an attorney, and I strongly advise none of you here to do this exercise!" For him and for us, he said warningly, this was asking for trouble with the tax authorities.

Let me begin by asking you what are your memories of how money was handled in your childhood? Are these good or bad memories?

Did it matter what sex a person was when it came to money in your family? Were men, for instance, supposed to know and care more? Women to be grateful? Or vice versa?

How did money move around within your family? Who controlled budgets? Was this control disputed at all?

Could money be talked about openly in your home?

Have you done "better" than your parents? If so, have there been any emotional problems over that? Yours, or theirs, or both? If you have not done "better", how do you feel about it?

This would be the monied version of Oedipus. I've done some empirical work on this. I sent questionnaires to a few clinicians at five-yearly intervals from 1992 to 2002 asking what clients were talking about in terms of political preoccupations and—as one might expect—one top theme was money and socio-economic status. Status can be understood as symbolising oedipal victory, or castration, or intergenerational mutual incomprehension. These themes are all stirred by this question of doing better (or not) than your parents. As I hinted earlier, movement is going to be downwards as well as upwards—in 2009, the *Guardian* carried a long article entitled "How Britain's middle class was betrayed" and the title says all I want to say about it at this point.

> How do you think you are doing in terms of handling money issues in your current relationship or family? Rate yourself on a scale of one to ten where one is very bad and ten is very good.

I have found myself using in the clinical context the workshop technique of getting the client to rate herself or himself on a scale of one to ten where one is hellishly awful and ten is productive and harmonious. Sometimes, individuals and couples have "bad money days" (Where it feels clinically appropriate, and if asked, I would reveal my own score to a client). What I'd like to see some discussion of is whether the ubiquity of financial dissatisfaction in dysfunctional middle class relationships is adequately understood as the result of problematic interpersonal dynamics. Isn't finance in and of itself a major cause of relationship distress? How might we address that clinically? Divorce lawyers or divorce mediators will probably have much to teach us here.

> When you fantasise having a lot of money, what are you doing with it? If you've never had such fantasies, try it right now!

Some answers to this question are benevolent and maybe ten per cent of those are true! What interests me is eliciting economic sadism. This is where I think we find the deal breaker, bar, or delimiter on our altruistic, benevolent, and idealistic economic aspirations. Most people have pretty nasty fantasies in the money zone, fantasies of getting rid of rivals, attaining superiority, eliminating awkward othernesses whenever they are encountered. In analysis, some, but surely not all, of this may emerge in the transference. But perhaps there is an ineluctable cruelty attached to money and this may be one area where "tragic vision" is all we can muster. Humans love their inequalities and that is that. On the other hand, with economic sadism brought to consciousness, economic benevolence (the term introduced in this context by Adam Smith, and which, as the polls tell us, sputters altruistically below the surface in Western polities) may flower as electoral support for fiscal and other programmes to reduce economic inequality.

Reflecting on our economic sadism. I think many of us were more complicit in the Great Crash of 2008 than we can bear to admit. At workshops on "the economic psyche", I ask participants to fantasise about the most shameful, sadistic, controlling, horrible thing they would do if they had a very large sum of money at their disposal—trillions of dollars. A professor of philosophy at the workshop in Pittsburgh said, "Well, if I had unlimited funds, I'd buy thousands of acres of skiing land at Aspen and fence it off so no one could use it." I did not think this was very sadistic, to say the least. Then he blurted out: "And I'd hire the US Marine Corps to machine-gun anyone who came near." He burst into tears and told us about his tycoon father and the relationship they had, and other personal information.

Shameful economic fantasy tells us how even people of progressive views are deeply invested in a system of economic injustice. If we want to change this system, we need to recognise what we are up against. It's about owning our own bit of the system, a piece of shadow from which we can all too glibly detach ourselves. The lesson is that economic sadism is not something you can escape just because you want to leap out of the pit.

I would like to be optimistic about the prospects for economic justice but, without a change in awareness and the backing of many groups—including analysts—for a new approach to economics, it will be hard to achieve change. What psychotherapists can contribute is the idea that economic injustice and economic inequality is bad for your mental health, bad for the soul, bad for the spirit.

The sooner we admit our economic crimes to others, to other peoples, creeds, genders, species, the better and lighter the human future will be. The more even the middle classes deny their economic sadism, the greater will be "the horrors and the vengeances of time that wait silently in the wings of the bloody dramas of our future", in Ben Okri's (1999) words. It's not just the hubris of the bankers. It's ours, too. Not being Odysseus, most of got seduced by the Circe of easy personal debt. How many credit cards are there in your purse or wallet? As the Baal Shem Tov put it, "Sinners are mirrors. When we see faults in them, we must realise they only reflect evil in us."

I think the valuing of equality, what I call democratic spirituality, is not dead in polities such as America or Britain. But time is running out.

Now, in the never-ending financial crisis, is the moment for us to call for an economic sacrifice on the part of developed countries and even on the part of the middle classes in such countries where there are millions below the poverty line. Hitting the rich is hard to do (though easy to justify), as we know. But I am talking about the economic sacrifices that could be made by millions of ordinary middle-class folk. And if this idea of economic sacrifice fits with what other people are saying about sustainability and global warming, so much the better.

I will conclude this section with a few ideas about sacrifice, with climate change and sustainable economics in mind. We know that people will make sacrifices for their children or for the sake of a cause they believe in, or in the hope of greater benefits in the future (what the economists call "opportunity costs"). But this is about sacrifice in and of itself, and the spontaneous meanings it can generate.

Sacrifice is a widespread psychological and historical theme. Sacrifice lies at the heart of the Abrahamic religions (the aborted sacrifice of Isaac) but is much, much older as a propitiation of the Gods. Asceticism has a long cultural history, as does martyrdom, including that of suicide bombers.

In Jungian psychology, reference is made to the sacrifice of the ego for the sake of a flowering of the wider personality in individuation (Neumann, 1954). In art and religion, we contemplate the sacrifice of autonomy and control to something experienced as "other", whether inside or outside the self. The next, and final experiential exercise, takes up this theme.

I ask you to recall times when giving something up produced an unexpected and wonderfully fulfilling experience. Or think of how you admire someone who has made a sacrifice. Thinking specifically about economic sacrifice, what sacrifice could you imagine yourself making? What sacrifices could you imagine your own country making?

Inheritance

Please hold those thoughts on sacrifice, economic and otherwise, in mind and now join me in a questioning psychotherapeutic engagement with the whole question of inherited wealth and the entire problematic of "estate".

The best way to get rich is to come from a rich family. You will do even better if your rich family live in a rich country. We need some psychotherapeutic exploration of the phenomenon of inherited wealth because, on both the individual/familial and the national levels, this lies at the heart of economic inequality and hence is implicated in misery, hopelessness, and death across the planet. As I will detail later, there are global gendered aspects to this, females suffering more than males.

I think there is still somewhat of a taboo on the analytic exploration of the phenomenon of inherited wealth as opposed to other matters from the past. Analysts need to be more personal about this, I feel. Without a legacy of £5,000 from my grandfather, I could not have afforded training analysis. I bet there are many with similar stories—not everyone, obviously, but enough to assemble a decent body of ideas about it.

Many of us have been the objects of inherited wealth (we got legacies, perhaps small ones, perhaps big ones, or maybe we didn't and have some feeling about it). And maybe all of us, in our different middle class or upper middle class or lower middle class or professional class ways, will be the subjects of it. What exactly do you want to do with your money when you die? What are your ideal fantasies about that matter? What are your more shameful and sadistic fantasies? How can we begin to open up the entire field of economic subject and object relations, leading to a consideration of economic intersubjectivity?

Inherited wealth is, of course, a very complex topic, politically as well as psychologically. Inherited wealth both contributes to intense social stratification and class polarisation, and has also been positioned as a way out of social impasse—for example, when minority ethnic groups start to leave wealth to their descendants, their social location changes (presumably, on this argument, for the better). It has been part of Jewish experience in Britain, for sure, and I imagine elsewhere. Reading accounts of what Michelle Obama said during the 2008 presidential election campaign about her income on a women-only TV show brought home to me how psychologically complex are processes of social mobility, structuration, class, and ethnicity. She had a rough time of it in the press.

Inherited wealth and its vicissitudes sits at the heart of the "human nature" debate—what is the relative balance between economic ruthlessness and sadism on the one hand, and economic altruism and compassion on the other? Taking a view on the proportions of economic selfishness and selflessness cannot be avoided if psychotherapy is to contribute to a whole range of economic policy issues ranging from taxation to the invisible movements of international finance claimed to be outside the control of elected governments. I mean, the obvious and cheap answer is "both". That isn't wrong but it is—how shall I put it?—a little disengaged.

Economics, gender, and ethnicity

My paternal grandfather was fantastic with money and, off the boat from Poland, made a lot. That's how I got the £5,000 for the training analysis. My father was much less good at it. My own financial incapacity is legendary. My elder son became an actor. It is interesting to consider how these differing generational monetary abilities affect (or do not affect) our intrapsychic conceptions of ourselves as men.

There are some special economic features to consider in terms of intrapsychic self-positioning as men. When I write that my financial incapacity is legendary, there is an ironic and assertive cast to it that is still definitely and defiantly (and suspiciously) "masculine" on my part. I win by losing, as we used to say in encounter groups. So only holy men and their vows of poverty are exceptions to the rule that men should do well economically. Aside from these kinds of subtleties, who can doubt that the Western (and maybe global) consensus is that the more money, the more manhood.

Now, this cultural consensus on the surface could not be further from what analysts and therapists learn from the depths in their consulting rooms. The hedge fund wizard with erectile dysfunction is, by now, a well-known clinical phenomenon, almost a cliché. Without going into his cross-dressing or submissive fantasy, there may even be a formula that says "the more external masculinity, the less internal confidence in it", or something like that. Economic success is understood by psychoanalysis as always already a psychic compensation. If you think it through psychotherapeutically, economic downturns and "the betrayal of the middle class man" may unconsciously be a huge psychological relief for men as well as, more obviously, a major stressor for them.

It is not hard to see the pickle therapists are in if we want to communicate exaggerated insights like these to the wider world! We'd have to risk ridicule. Or would we? Don't millions of people know that there's a toddler within the tycoon, and that the tycoon isn't always good for the toddler? More academically, there's by now a huge body of work (the main player being Richard Wilkinson, mentioned earlier) that shows how major quality of life indicators (e.g., infant mortality, life expectancy, epidemiological factors including mental health) do not stem from poverty as such but, as measured in the thirty richest countries, from the degree of economic inequality therein.

Psychoanalysts and psychotherapists speak fluently about sex difference and gender politics but have perhaps left relational economics to the social scientists. Work done by social scientists on, for example, the psychological difficulties faced by long-term unemployed men in the rustbelts of Western countries is relevant to our ordinary clinical work— to quote Muriel Dimen: "studying social disorder reveals instead the normal lines of discontinuity and conflict that are the fault lines along which cultural evolution and changes in inner life occur" (1994, p. 75).

If I were a woman, I am not sure where I'd stand regarding the oft-stated idea that I might be less rigid (and hence maybe less greedy and more "relational") when it comes to money matters. I have no idea whether it is true or not that such a difference from a generic man exists. When we explore such things, it all becomes extremely complex. Class (or structuration) analyses interweave with gender issues and the resultant mélange comes through in the clinical situation.

My clinical experience with some female clients is that money issues and aggression issues are linked and that fantasies in the one area turn out to be also of the other area. Winning the lottery and revenge upon the parents co-symbolise. Yet I find it much easier to work with a woman's aggressive fantasies, including in the transference, than I ever do with her monetary fantasies. Is this just me, or me as a typical man? Or am I picking something up of more interest? What do women want, when it comes to money? *How much* does a woman want?!

We know what women *get*, even if we may not know what they want. The global economic system is murderous to women and children, as Amartya Sen has taught us. His article "Woman's survival as a development problem" (1989) was one of a number of brilliant and instructive examples of a gender-aware approach to economics leading to his conclusion that 100,000,000 women have gone "missing".

We know what women *don't* get, which is the same pay for the same work (all statistical indicators, even in Scandinavia, show this). The usual explanations concern pregnancy, motherhood, and career—how they just don't go together. And, in Britain at least, we have seen a growing moral panic—in which doctors, clergy, and many psychotherapists join—over mothers of young children who work, and this comes through with numerous clients.

Maybe this is the very best moment to bring back the thinking that 1970s and 1980s feminism generated about why it is taken for granted that unpaid work (in the home, for example, or volunteer work, or caring work) is somehow not part of the economy. Wages for housework or childcare might not cost as much as the manifold Wall Street and Detroit bailouts.

When Brazil's President Lula stated on 26 March 2009 that the economic crash was the responsibility of "white men with blue eyes", and that black people were the victims, many were shocked. Yet Lula added a necessary ethnic dimension to that of gender which we have been discussing. He is saying that it was whiteness that developed the mind-body split, global warming, unsustainable economics, nuclear technology, and free market economics. Whiteness got the bonus. It is whiteness that can contemplate brown and black people dying as if they mattered less than white people—they get killed these days in a kind of video arcade by unpiloted drones steered from underground chambers thousands of miles away back home in the States. For sure, race and ethnicity play out in myriad ways according to history and cultural context. But we have to contend with this constant whiteness, American whiteness, Western whiteness—the box we are in as I mentioned in Chapter One. These whitenesses have been allowed to become essentialised, universalised, removed from history.

I said that, in our clinical work, therapists understand how clients have to struggle to stop thinking like their parents. In our political work, maybe we could experiment with trying to stop thinking like a nation or like a state. In order to claim the freedom to stop thinking like the state, we have to make sacrifices—a sacrifice of identity, security, and having one's feet on the ground in a place called home. It's time to leave home, to get outside the box, and press for a relational economics. To do this, we have to make some sacrifices: sacrifices in which we act to lose home, suspend identity, refuse the offer of security—in the yearning hope of finding them—home, identity, security—once again.

Money, soul, and spirit

I composed this final section in an attempt to discover the more beautiful aspects of economic activity. Reviewing my text, I found it to be a bit too downbeat, too tragic, even sentimentally so. Maybe it has not been read that way, obviously I cannot know. But I just can't see how something as ubiquitous and universal as economic activity can only be bad! It'd be like saying sex is bad …

Islamic conceptions of and rules for economic activity are extremely interesting from a psychological point of view. Not for the first time, I have found utility and inspiration in what Muslim writers have to say about pressing issues for us in the West. In Chapter Two, I wrote about the idea of ta'aruf, a Qur'anic idea in which conflict between groups of people, nations, and even the sexes is understood to have been created by Allah so that people can get to know one another better. Ta'aruf means "that you shall come to know one another". I found that much psychoanalytic theorising on aggression parallels this idea of ta'aruf.

Similarly, in terms of the economy, there is increased discussion these days of what is involved in Sharia-compliant banking in which the earning of interest is forbidden. Central to Islamic finance is the fact that money itself has no intrinsic value. As a matter of faith, a Muslim cannot lend money to, or receive money from, someone and expect to benefit—interest (known as riba) is not allowed. To make money from money is forbidden—wealth can only be generated through legitimate trade and investment in assets. Money must be used in a productive way. The principal means of Islamic finance are based on trading—it is essential that risk be involved in any trading activity. Any gains relating to the trading are shared between the person providing the capital and the person providing the expertise.

Now, I am not sure that we need to share totally in this moral repudiation of money by Islam, suggestive and fascinating though it is. For there is something to recuperate in Western conceptions of money. The etymology of the English word "money" is that it stems from the Latin moneta which was also the name (Moneta) the Romans used for Mnemosyne, memory and the mother of the Muses. The deeper root is mens which means conscience, reason, and rationality. Money as suggesting conscience, reason, rationality? How amazing. Something certainly has got lost concerning money in the West, and not only in translation!

And now something from my own tradition, the Jewish idea of Pe-ah. The passage in Leviticus (19:9–10) reads "And when you reap the harvest of your land, you shall not reap to the very corners of your field [pe'ot means corners], nor shall you gather the gleanings of your harvest."

Sure, there is much to question when it comes to economic charity and philanthropy, and who wants to live on gleanings and grain from the corners? Generosity often masks misanthropy, as we see in Shakespeare's *Timon of Athens*, when Timon takes a terrible sadistic revenge, somehow already there inside him, when the friends he has helped financially let him down in his hour of need.

It is supercilious and disengaged for the psychotherapist to sit in judgement on humanity, balancing the positive and the negative notions of human nature that arise when we consider economic matters. I remain optimistic and hopeful. Whether it is via Sharia, or via a recuperation of deeper and more wholesome associations to money, or via Leviticus, or by a passionate engagement in therapy, there is something in the economic psyche that offers us the chance to travel hopefully on the road to utopia, pick up what we need, then trudge back again.

What if, on this trudging journey, we do manage a change or transformation in the economic psyche, do make the economic sacrifices we know are needed? Listen to what John Maynard Keynes, whose name is again on everyone's lips these days, had to say about it in 1930 in "Economic possibilities for our grandchildren":

> [W]e shall use the new-found bounty of nature quite differently from the way the rich use it to-day, and will map out a plan of life quite otherwise than theirs. ... [W]hat work there still remains to be done will be as widely shared as possible. ... There will be great changes in the code of morals. ... I see us free ... to return to some of the most sure and certain principles of religion and traditional virtue—that avarice is a vice, that the exaction of usury is a misdemeanour, and the love of money is detestable ... We shall honour those who can teach us how to pluck the hour and the day virtuously and well, the delightful people who are capable of taking direct enjoyment in things. (Keynes, 1930, pp. 368–372)

By now, we have to speak of Keynes' great grandchildren and great-great grandchildren. These generations face many of the same huge economic problems that he tried to address. But there is by now a new tinge to these problems—that of sustainability, responses to climate change, and the field of endeavour known as ecopsychology. These themes form the core of the next chapter.

CHAPTER FOUR

Against nature*

As you will see, in 1993 I utilised a nineteenth-century French novel (*Against Nature*) set against Atwood's late twentieth-century "environmental" novel (*Surfacing*) to make salient points about a change of tone (at the very least) I felt was needed in environmental discourse. I stand by what I wrote and feel that those of us concerned with climate change and sustainability face many of the same problems—and, in a way, we remain the main problem.

At an ecopsychology conference in 2009, I gave a workshop also entitled "Against nature". In it, I put the point I'd first made in 1993. If environmentalists (as we called them then) want to be effective than they

---

*This chapter is a slightly revised (updated) version of a chapter from my 1993 book *The Political Psyche*. At that time, the scientific and political debate over climate change was more evenly balanced than it is now. But little else has changed—even the deposing of the human being as the centre of everything in Margaret Atwoood's novel *Surfacing* (1972a) anticipates similar perspectives today. The ideas in the chapter got me into a lot of trouble with political allies and comrades because people didn't recognise it was written from a viewpoint that actually supported the environmental movement. Yet I did feel that there was (and I think that there still is) an unsound idealisation of nature going on that could be destructive in terms of effective and consistent politics.

need to stop blaming people for ruining the world or turning a blind eye to its ruination. Fantasies of being destructive and of destroying that which one loves and needs lie at the heart of depressive anxiety; and depressive anxiety involves paralysis of action and will. Ergo, we need to find other ways to get the political result.

I argued that what we now call ecopsychology fails to celebrate the urban and the cosmopolitan, fails to understand that artifice is natural for humans. In order to deepen this thought experientially, in the workshop, I distributed sample phials of many perfumes that Selfridges very kindly gave me. In pairs and threes, participants used the perfumes, applied them to each other, and compared notes. It was a smelly old exercise and a lot of fun.

Before the exercise, I asked who in the audience of around ninety-five ecopsychologists wore perfume or its male equivalents. Only one person said that she did. Who read fashion magazines in which perfumes are widely advertised? None, though one person said guiltily that she did it in the dentist's waiting room. I said that this showed why environmentalism would fail and why ecopsychology had truncated itself. For those in the room—I arrogantly excepted myself!—had got completely cut off from ordinary urban life—the life of the piazza, I called it.

I am as frightened of the destruction of the planet as many people in the ecopsychology world, I think. But I am also convinced that, if you look in the right way, there is much of value in the fripperies of fashion and consumerism and it is elitist to deny that. Depth lying hidden on the surface (to use words from Atwood's novel).

In this chapter, I discuss environmentalism and ecopsychology and ask: must these movements fail? I suggest they will fail unless they become more conscious of the authoritarianism and depression within them, and the idealisation of nature is somehow moderated.

Criticisms of the authoritarianism of the environmental movement, referring to its "eco-terrorism", could wreck it by playing into the hands of entrenched industrial and financial institutions. I think we should begin by admitting that there is a degree of accuracy in such criticisms. For there is a hidden authoritarianism in much of the new ecological politics, which sometimes seem to be the latest manifestation of belief in perfectibility. Whether this takes the form of a downgrading of humanity to the level of fauna (or flora) or the issuing of a whole set of edicts about what is "good", the tendency is clear to see. And already a backlash is going on. I think that environmentalist authoritarianism stems from a deeply buried misanthropy and, unless challenged, will itself turn out to be secretly and horrendously destructive. In Jungian terms, this is the shadow of the ecological movement and it would be helpful to become more conscious of it. Then the advantages of the unquenchable human thirst for a better world can be enjoyed—for only things of substance cast a shadow.

Casting an analyst's eye over the information and education material put out by organisations such as Greenpeace and Friends of the Earth, I am struck by the one-sided portrait of humanity that is presented. Certainly, there is much to feel guilty about, much thoughtlessness and destructive behaviour to be owned, much acquiescence in horrid developments to be confessed. But the unremitting litany of humanity's destructiveness may not be the way to spur movement in a more creative direction. The result of too much self-disgust may be the cultivation of a deadening cultural depression that would interfere with environmental action. This is because, as I mentioned, fantasies of being all-bad and all-destructive usually lie at the heart of depressive illness. Therefore environmentalists should try to avoid any presentation of ideas about the environment that reflects humanity in an exclusively harsh light.

Instead, they might also celebrate what careful tending of the earth there has been over millennia. They might reaffirm the goodness, gentleness, and aesthetic sensibility of humanity's artificial, cultural productions—our buildings, cities, art works, and so forth. As an instance of what I am talking about, I think of the continuity to be found in the relations between humans and the environment in England. There is a sense in which the landscape itself has been made and remade over time as each succeeding generation leaves its mark. Emphasising this cultural layering means that a more positive estimation of our environmental potential is brought into being.

It is vital not to represent environmentalism as a concern of the privileged classes, cut off from wider issues of social justice. To begin with, we have already seen that the greening of politics is going to be painful, both within Western societies and in terms of the relations between the developed and the undeveloped worlds. A whole host of moral decisions arises when we in the industrially advanced countries call for limits on deforestation in poor countries or advocate that they control their birthrates. We need an educational programme that confronts people with these decisions and choices rather than experts being allowed to make those choices for them, thereby offering people protection from the moral implications of what is being done. Otherwise we will end up with a new Western hegemony: we will be okay but the poor of the earth will be even worse off.

What is more, we should not look to things such as "ethical" changes in consumer spending patterns to bring about improvement. Are we to say that when the going gets tough the greens go shopping? If substantive issues of social justice are not addressed then we will just be doing a landscaping job.

The question of economic redistribution within advanced societies is going to have to be addressed. If the polluters are to pay, then prices will rise enormously. The knock-on effects will be dramatic and many goods that we take for granted will be priced out of reach. I want to suggest that this is a marvellous opportunity! We are going to have to think about how we live and about how resources are distributed within our more advanced societies—and this will mean challenging the awesome power structures that exist. The problems confronting the world force a critical engagement with the banks, the multinational corporations, the IMF, and with governments.

Calls for a return to traditional forms of homeworking or the setting up of *ersatz* agrarian-style communities should be treated with caution. For, in such situations, the lot of women has been and would continue to be an unhappy one. Instead, we should think of greening the cities we already have, making them safer and more pleasant for the groups they oppress—women, children, the elderly. For it has never been demonstrated that agrarian, parochial life is inherently superior to urban, cosmopolitan life. Advocating the tearing down of cities so as to foster the triumph of nature would be the way of a Khmer Vert.

Our young people will see through any educational campaign that idealises nature, leaving out its frightening, harsh, and bloody aspects and our ambivalence toward it. Such a campaign would resemble those commissioned portraits of the eighteenth century in which the lady of the manor is pictured dressed up as a milkmaid. The effect was to make nature an acceptable decorative element in the salons of the rich. Nature is itself not "natural" but a culturally constructed idea. Moreover, the environmental movement still has to work on a balance between its "anthropocentric" middle-of-the-roaders and its extreme wing—sometimes called "ecologism". Are we doing this for ourselves, for our own benefit and that of our children and other humans? Or is that simply a new gloss on the old exploitative attitude to nature? Should we not be acting for the benefit of an entire planetary organism? Battle lines are even now being drawn up between green extremists and the rest of the community, including "ordinary" environmentalists. The argument that trees and rivers have rights needs to be assessed so that we can distinguish between its potential to inspire action and its gross oversimplifications. Does the HIV virus have "rights"? Is it ethical to destroy dams or insert into trees spikes that injure loggers?

In this chapter, I will question some of the underlying assumptions and practices of the modern environmental movement by exploring the tensions between nature and artifice revealed by a critical comparison of two very different yet somehow complementary novels that seem to mark out this particular patch of psychological, cultural, and socio-economic territory. The novels are Margaret Atwood's *Surfacing* (1972) and J. -K. Huysmans's *Against Nature* (*À Rebours*, 1884). The interplay between Huysmans's hymn to artifice and Atwood's celebration of a woman's journey to a profound encounter with nature turns out to have political and social resonances. Certainly, these are very different books. But they both engage with the idea of nature, they both present definite though complicated visions of sexuality, and they were both written at times when the relations between humanity and industrialism, and between women and men, were displaying rapid changes. Atwood was writing at the beginning of contemporary feminism, during the Nixon era with the Vietnam War in progress. Huysmans was working in the ferment of Paris in the 1880s, a time when the functions and forms of art were undergoing the most radical revision. Yet Huysmans, whom one would have thought of as the quintessential Artist (with a capital A), spent his entire working life in a government office and, in retirement, attempted to join a Trappist monastery. I hope the books can indeed bear the burden I am placing upon them. However, the chapter is more than a literary critique of two novels.

I assume that readers are broadly familiar with the current debate associated with environmentalism: the possibility of global warming, deforestation, and species depletion, damaging of the ozone layer, acid rain and other pollutions, the limits to growth, the need for sus-tainable growth, the debate about population limitation, the general decay of urban civilisation. I assume, too, an awareness of the gap in wealth between the industrially advanced countries and the develop-ing countries, with the latter group heavily in debt to the former and often economically dominated by global corporations based in the industrially advanced countries. The tensions between the two kinds of country have been written about so often that, allowing for differences of opinion, most readers will be aware that many developing countries assert their own right to the technological and industrial features that provide the consumers of the developed world with all their goodies. It is all very well for the industrially advanced countries to worry about pollution or deforestation in the developing countries but there is a certain irony in the fact that those who protest about what is happening to the rain forests of Amazonia themselves live in countries that consume a disproportionate amount of the earth's resources. In 1986 the United States was the only country to vote against the Declaration on the Right to Development passed in the General Assembly of the United Nations, and at the Earth Summit of 1992 the United States was also out of step with the rest of the world. This situation has scarcely changed.

I am sure I am not the only one to be bewildered by the competing claims of groups of scientists that the situation is very grave indeed, or that it is grave but not disastrous, or that the warnings of planetary collapse are greatly exaggerated. It was partly to think my way through a thicket of information that I began the work that now forms this chapter.

Surfacing

Margaret Atwood's *Surfacing* (1972) is presented in the first person. The anonymous narrator is returning to the northern bush lands of Canada because she has been informed of the mysterious disappearance of her father. She is a city-based commercial artist who has lost touch with her family and has not been home for many years. Sometime previously, she has left her marriage and child, and is travelling with three companions: a couple, Dave and Anna, and her lover, Joe. Dave and Joe are supposedly making a film in a *cinéma verité* style. The four are depicted, not uncritically but also with humour, as creatures of the late 1960s or early 1970s, with the typical linguistic affectations and cobbled-together values of the middle-class rebels of that era. However, the novel's repeated mention of "Americans" is not simply to be taken literally. "Americans" are signifiers of all that is crass, destructive of natural beauty, and threatening. This is a particularly Canadian referent, connected to Atwood's concern over the fate of Canadian culture and letters shown in another book of hers also published in 1972—a book of literary criticism entitled *Survival*. Moreover, as we saw, today's environmentalism has to deal with its own literal and metaphorical "Americans".

Drawing a blank at the homestead of an old farmer who was the narrator's father's best friend, the group of companions take a boat to the isolated cabin on an island in the lake in which the narrator had lived with her mother and father (her mother is dead). At the cabin, there is still no clue about what has happened to her father but, instead of returning to the city, the group decides to stay on for a further week, a decision which the narrator at first does not like. She organises the others so that they can live relatively comfortably in the deliberately simple domestic arrangements her father has chosen. She takes them on blueberry-picking and fishing trips and, in general, acts as a kind of wilderness guide for the other three.

All the while, she is studying her mother's photograph albums and the scrapbooks she and her brother had assembled. She is swamped by memories. Then she finds some drawings that her father has made. These are crude representations of human-like, exotic creatures. She concludes from the drawings, and his comments on them, that her father had gone mad. She is forced to change this view when she finds a letter from an anthropologist regarding material her father had collected and sent to him on ancient Indian rock paintings in the locality. The drawings must be of these paintings. She realises by now that her father is probably dead but is impelled to make use of a map she has found that seems to indicate the whereabouts of the rock paintings.

She goes out on to the lake and dives beneath the surface, for the map shows that some of the paintings are under water due to a rise in the surface level of the lake. There she finds, not a rock drawing, but her father's body, weighed down by his heavy camera. However, in the shock of that moment, she confuses his swollen and waterlogged body with the foetus she had aborted many years before when her then lover, her teacher and about the same age as her father, convinced her to get rid of the baby:

> It was there but it wasn't a painting, it wasn't on the rock. It was below me, drifting toward me from the furthest level where there was no life, a dark oval trailing limbs. It was blurred but it had eyes, they were open, it was something I knew about, a dead thing, it was dead.

> ... it was in a bottle curled up, staring out at me like a cat pickled; it had huge jelly eyes and fins instead of hands, fish gills. I couldn't let it out, it was dead already, it had drowned in air. (Atwood, 1972a, p. 143)

Following this catalytic experience, the narrator begins a *nekyia*, a kind of descent, in which she seeks to reverse her acculturation and attain a state of merger with nature. She persuades Joe to impregnate her, but does it in a way marked out as a meaningful ritual, an initiation rite.

> We go over the ground, feet and skin bare; the moon is rising, in the greygreen light his body gleams and the trunks of trees, the white ovals of his eyes. He walks as though blind, blundering into the shadow clumps, toes stubbing, he has not yet learned to see in the dark. My tentacled feet and free hand scent out the way ...
>
> I lie down, keeping the moon on my left hand and the absent sun on my right. He kneels, he is shivering, the leaves under and around us are damp from the dew, or is it the lake, soaking up through the rock and sand, we are near the shore, the small waves riffle. He needs to grow more fur. (Atwood, 1972a, p. 161)

By now the narrator has disappeared from the sight of her companions who return to the city in frustration. Acting on implicit knowledge that she is on some kind of significant journey, the narrator sinks into, embraces, and identifies with the earth and its animals, with nature.

> Something has happened to my eyes, my feet are released, they alternate, several inches from the ground. I'm ice-clear, transparent, my bones and the child inside me showing through the green webs of my flesh, the ribs are shadows, the muscles jelly, the trees are like this too, they shimmer, their cores glow through the wood and bark.
>
> The forest leaps upward, enormous, the way it was before they cut it, columns of sunlight frozen; the boulders float, melt, everything is made of water, even the rocks. In one of the languages there are no nouns, only verbs held for a longer moment.
>
> The animals have no need for speech, why talk when you are a word.
>
> I lean against a tree, I am a tree leaning.

I break out again into the bright sun and crumple, head against
the ground.

I am not an animal or a tree, I am the thing in which the trees
and animals move and grow, I am a place. (Atwood, 1972a, p. 181)

Right at the end of *Surfacing*, Joe returns on his own to look for her and,
like an inquisitive but cautious beast, she watches him from the trees.
The frame freezes.

Perhaps more than any other single artistic production of the past
forty or so years, *Surfacing* deepened and highlighted questions about
the cultural and psychological linkages of women and nature. These
questions have mainly been taken up in two contradictory ways. First,
as referring us to a power and knowledge of nature held exclusively by
women, based on their reproductive and nurturing capacities. Thus,
women are the true guardians of nature, creatures of the earth god-
desses, emblems and purveyors of all that is fecund. The second view
is that the equation of women and nature is one of the main processes
that bind women into their oppressed place in patriarchal culture. For,
as the subjugation of nature by (male) science proceeds, the subjugation of women, equated with nature, will proceed in parallel. *Surfacing*
appears, superficially, to come down on the side of the first viewpoint,
supporting and celebrating a twinning of woman and nature. But, as
we will see, it is not as straightforward as that and *Surfacing* is not at all
an essentialist tract.

It is interesting that, in the intense debate between feminist circles
over these issues that were and are highlighted by *Surfacing*, there has
been (quite rightly, in my view) very little space for the facile line beloved
of the rote Jungians that at-oneness with nature is a "feminine" capacity
or quality, meaning a femininity capable of being developed internally
by any woman or man. This metaphorical femininity is not the theme
of *Surfacing*, nor the basis of what has been termed "eco-feminism"—
the perspective that sees correspondences between a despoiled planet
and the exploited and ravished female body. The equation of women
and nature, whether taken as an indication of female potential and
female gifts, or as an indicator of culturally driven female inferiority,
cannot be split off from flesh-and-blood women.

Of course, there are many layers in a polysemous novel such as
Surfacing and, as Francine du Plessix Gray (1972, p. 6) says, "Atwood's
genius rises above these debates". However, I do not agree with du

Plessix Gray that the novel has to be taken as a religious quest or as the working out of a female religious vision or, as other critics have claimed, as part of a typical, "Jungian", "individuation" process, following the "archetypal" stages of a (or the) shamanic journey. Undoubtedly, the narrator does go through a transformative process in which psychologically heightened exposure to the material world of her childhood functions so as to transcend the materiality of that childhood and, indeed, the materiality of the physical world itself. But this is quite specifically a transformation downward: down into the lake, down into the animal world, down (if you will) into the unconscious. This journey downward involves the narrator in nothing less than a transcendence of her human body:

> the footprints are there, side by side in the mud. My breath quickens, it was true, I saw it. But the prints are too small, they have toes; I place my feet in them and find they are my own.
>   I am part of the landscape, I could be anything, a tree, a deer skeleton, a rock. (Atwood, 1972a, p. 187)

Transcending the body, and doing it downwards not upwards towards spiritual planes, implies a transcendence of ego-consciousness itself, or rather an assumption of a kind of "natural" consciousness, a fathomless nature consciousness—so that there is a paradox of total unconsciousness acting as a phantasmagoric consciousness. It is a paradox we have met before, when we met the Trickster who challenges the habitual division: below, matter; above, spirit.

Let us review the particular features of the narrator's transformations: the downward moves to an embrace with inferiority, the absolute bodily fluidity, the naive but magical omnipotence, the unconsciousness that is revealed as a treasure-chest of natural consciousness, even the ambiguous ending of the book (will she, can she go to Joe or not?).

The oft-discussed (and spurious) equation of women and nature now takes on yet another set of implications. It ceases to be a question posed in terms either of the celebration of women or of the subjugation of women. The equation of women and nature is revealed as having as its goal or *telos* nothing less than the social transformation of women. In Atwood's words:

[The Americans] can't be trusted. They'll mistake me for a human being, a naked woman wrapped in a blanket: possibly that's what they've come here for, if it's running around loose, ownerless, why not take it. They won't be able to tell what I really am. But if they guess my true form, identity, they will shoot me or bludgeon in my skull and hang me up by the feet from a tree. (Atwood, 1972a, p. 183)

This is a deep trick because a woman who is by now not a woman but really an animal is pretending to be a woman lest in her true form she be treated as an animal by American men who have come to hunt in the Canadian wilderness. The female narrator of *Surfacing* quite literally "drops out". Ceasing to be a woman, she cannot be subjugated like nature because she is nature. But, to the extent that nature threatens people, especially men like Joe, or Americans, as a woman still she acquires nature's deathly powers—woman as "Ice Woman", to use a phrase from Atwood's other book *Survival* (1972b). But we know it is still an illusion, because men still have the "real" power, the socioeconomic power, the political power. It is no accident that, in the carefully crafted ghost story that is *Surfacing*, Atwood assigns all the pioneering skills—fishing, fire-making, tracking—to a female.

Reflecting upon the image of the female Trickster as agent of political change, especially of change in our attitudes to and dealings with the environment, offers an opportunity to break away from those three problems I mentioned at the beginning of the chapter: authoritarianism, depression, and an idealisation of nature. Environmentalism is itself subjected to a critique modelled on the upside-downness of the Trickster.

The trick is to use the most eternal, the most "natural" formulation but to orientate that usage in the direction of social change. The eternal points up the mutable. Atwood is neither extolling woman as nature nor critiquing the notion: she is using it to reinforce a political project. The power of nature is, as we say, harnessed—but under a different aegis than that of phallogocentric industrialism controlled by "Americans".

Atwood's concern with the survival of Canadian letters in the face of American cultural imperialism needs to be brought back into the picture. The relationship between the novel *Surfacing* and the critical work *Survival* is an extraordinarily complex one, not least in Atwood's own mind. But I think it is justifiable to propose that *Surfacing* is part of a response to the political problem of cultural and environmental survival depicted in *Survival*. In her critical book, Atwood points up the difference between "nature as woman" and "woman as nature". As one who is both poet and novelist, she tells us that prose writers incline toward "woman as nature", thereby confirming, if in code, that it is women on whom she wishes to focus in the prose work *Surfacing*. Hence, perhaps, these lines:

> This above all, to refuse to be a victim. Unless I can do that I can do nothing, I have to recant, give up the old belief that I am power-less and because of it nothing I can do will ever hurt anyone. A lie which was always more disastrous than the truth would have been. (Atwood, 1972a, p. 191)

Nature and anxiety

Woman as nature makes many of us anxious. Yet, on the cultural level, the equation of woman and nature may itself be seen as a response to anxiety. In his seminal book, *Man and the Natural World*, Keith Thomas (1983) argued that the snowball of industrialism, Enlightenment, and modernity created a profound anxiety in European cultural consciousness, to the point of neurosis, over what was being done by civilised humans to the natural world. Between 1500 and 1800, massive doubts emerged over the changes brought about by science and technology in the ways the natural world was perceived. There were many expressions of this counter-cultural sentiment. Theologians altered their notions about the relations between humanity and the rest of creation so as to gentle those relations and accommodate a certain decentring of humanity. Naturalists tried to understand and classify other species in non-anthropomorphic terms, thereby respecting their separate existence. Scientists explored links between humans and animals. Moral philosophers urged kindness to animals. In the city, the land came to be regarded as a thing of beauty, fit for contemplation, not as a useful resource. In sum, by 1800, people had responded to the anxiety engendered by the brutalising path on which the world seemed embarked. The list of cultural and intellectual developments I have cited is evidence of the anxiety-driven shift in consciousness.

Today's concerns over the limits to growth, animal welfare, and the fate of the environment may be regarded as descended from these earlier expressions of cultural anxiety. Yet we should temper our admiration for those who could not stomach "progress". They did not actually stop its march. Today, animal experimentation and factory-farming have to coexist with the supreme idealisation of the animal: the child's toy furry animal. As Thomas says, these cuddly creatures "enshrine the values by which society as a whole cannot afford to live"—an observation he extends to include nature parks and conservation areas (p. 301).

The revolution in consciousness that Thomas writes about constituted a kind of underground resistance to what was being done to the natural world. This resistance went beyond a reaction to the ruination of nature. The perception of slaves, non-Europeans, children, and women also underwent profound changes. As far as women were concerned, the form that liberal anxiety about modernity's denigration of women took was of an oppressive (and convenient) idealisation that restricted women to private and domestic roles. The idealisation of women and the idealisation of nature share similar roots in cultural history in the West: they are both reaction formations. But women and nature remain deeply threatening because the idealisations of them are based on such flimsy and anxiety-ridden foundations. Hence the swiftness with which the image of the "natural" woman moves from one who soothes a crying child or makes beds neatly into one who, transparent and web-footed, gazes at the man she commanded to fertilise her from behind a screen of trees.

So the cult of the countryside has this she-demon at its heart. Gaia tips over into the Terrible Mother and the proud, human illusion of serving as Gaia's physicians is replaced by the starker reality of our being her slavish attendants, her Cabiri.

Against Nature

Any difficulty with summarising the plot of *Surfacing* fades into insignificance compared with having to summarise the plot of *Against Nature*.

Duc Jean Floressas des Esseintes admits that he suffers from *une névrose*, a neurosis. At the age of thirty—Atwood was thirty-three when she wrote *Surfacing*—des Esseintes, the scion of a degenerated aristocratic family, decides to leave the debauched, big-city life of Paris and retreat to a "desert equipped with all modern conveniences, a snugly heated ark on dry land in which he might take refuge from the incessant deluge of human stupidity". We are told that, try what he might, he could not shake off the overpowering tedium which weighed upon him. In desperation he had recourse to "the perilous caresses of the professional virtuosos, but the only effect was to impair his health and exacerbate his nerves" (Huysmans, 1884, p. 64).

Even prior to his move, des Esseintes has a reputation as an eccentric. For example, he gave the by-now notorious "black banquet", a dinner modelled on a funeral feast:

> The dining room, draped in black, opened out into a garden metamorphosed for the occasion, the paths being strewn with charcoal, the ornamental pond edged with black basalt and filled with ink, the shrubberies replanted with cypresses and pines. The dinner itself was served on a black cloth adorned with baskets of violets and scabious; candelabra shed an eerie green light over the table and tapers flickered in the chandeliers.
>
> While a hidden orchestra played funeral marches, the guests were waited on by naked negresses wearing only slippers and stockings in cloth of silver embroidered with tears.
>
> Dining off black-bordered plates, the company had enjoyed turtle soup, Russian rye bread, ripe olives from Turkey, caviare, mullet botargo, black puddings from Frankfurt ...
>
> On the invitations, which were similar to those sent out before more solemn obsequies, this dinner was described as a funeral banquet in memory of the host's virility, lately but only temporarily deceased. (Huysmans, 1884, p. 83)

By the way, thinking of those invitations, Huysmans made up des Esseintes's name from railway timetables to avoid the possibility of being sued for libel.

Having constructed his retreat, des Esseintes sets out to lead a life devoted to the experience of the highest forms of artifice and artificiality. Using the finest and most expensive materials, he builds for himself a replica of a monk's cell in which he will sleep. The point is that great expense is employed to create the appearance of humble poverty. Des Esseintes also constructs what he calls his "mouth organ", a machine that dispenses liqueurs in tiny quantities, thus permitting a kind of blending to go on within the blender's own mouth:

> The organ was then open. The stops labelled "flute", "horn", and "vox angelica" were pulled out, ready for use. Des Esseintes would drink a drop here, another there, playing internal symphonies to himself, and providing his palate with sensations analogous to those which music dispenses to the ear.
>
> Indeed, each and every liqueur, in his opinion, corresponded in taste with the sound of a particular instrument. ...
>
> Once these principles had been established ... he even succeeded in transferring specific pieces of music to his palate. (Huysmans, 1884, p.143)

Surrounding himself with exotic hot-house flowers, specially chosen for giving the appearance of being artificial flowers, des Esseintes spends many hours blending perfumes, seeking to reproduce, by artificial means, exact replicas of natural odours: "One aspect of the art of perfumery fascinated him more than any other, and that was the degree of accuracy it was possible to reach in imitating the real thing" (Huysmans, 1884, p. 196).

If des Esseintes wants to travel to London, he does not actually go there. He constructs a room on gimbals that reproduces artificially the rolling motions of the cross-Channel ferry and he has his servants make splashing sounds with barrels of salt water outside the window, using fans to waft in the salty smell. He travels to Paris so as to eat English food in an English restaurant, claiming that this is as "real" as doing it in London. He wears a fur coat in hot weather, forcing himself to shiver, admires the convolutions of decadent Latin poetry, adores the play of gorgeous colours on his walls, and praises the marvels of modern manufacture above all the works of nature in a passage that is surely the ideological heart of the book:

> Nature, he used to say, has had her day; she has finally and utterly exhausted the patience of sensitive observers by the revolting uniformity of her landscapes and skyscapes.
>
> ... In fact, there is not a single one of her inventions, deemed so subtle and sublime, that human ingenuity cannot manufacture. ...

There can be no shadow of doubt that with her never-ending platitudes the old crone has by now exhausted the good-humoured admiration of all true artists, and the time has surely come for artifice to take her place whenever possible.

After all, to take what among all her works is considered to be the most exquisite, what among all her creations is deemed to possess the most perfect and original beauty—to wit, woman—has not man, for his part, by his own efforts, produced an animate yet artificial creature that is every bit as good from the point of view of plastic beauty? Does there exist, anywhere on this earth, a being conceived in the joys of fornication and born in the throes of motherhood who is more dazzlingly, more outstandingly beautiful than the two locomotives recently put into service on the Northern Railway? (Huysmans, 1884, p. 111)

I have given what must necessarily be a partial list of the things des Esseintes gets up to in the privacy of his own home. Perhaps the *pièce de resistance* is des Esseintes's adoption of a system of rectal feeding by means of peptone enemas. He fantasises about all manner of delicious meals that might be consumed in this way. Thus, by artifice, basic biology is transcended.

How are we to understand des Esseintes's story, almost one hundred and fifty years later? We have our own malaises with which to contend. Certainly, he acts with a directed energy quite foreign to his enervated and dilapidated physical state. He acts strongly so that his weaknesses may be pursued—the enemas were actually recommended by his doctor as a last resort for his drastically failing health. Des Esseintes, as I understand him, is merely doing something *natural* by creating an *artificial* culture for himself; for making culture is "natural" for humans. Huysmans's genius is to hold a mirror up to ourselves, to disabuse us of the notion that we can separate nature from culture—and, thinking thoughts that hark back to *Surfacing*, to disabuse us of the notion that we can clearly separate so-called feminine (i.e., natural) and so-called masculine (i.e., cultural) capacities.

For sure, des Esseintes is not made happy by his experiment. Torn by vicious nightmares, he contemplates a return to the Catholic Church. In the ecclesiastic yearnings of des Esseintes, the Trickster artificer expresses his religious instinct—just as "I", the narrator in *Surfacing*, apparently on a religious quest, expressed her Trickster self.

Des Esseintes bears a message for our epoch about the ambivalence towards, and fear of, nature that no environmentalism can disguise. His neurosis is not merely a personal condition but a symbol of a collective crisis. Des Esseintes is both terrified of the body and seemingly quite at home with its febrile gestures. His mouth organ and his perfumery show that, within his own self-designated limits, he remains a perfectly sensual man. Moreover, throughout *Against Nature*, in his diatribes against nature, do we not hear des Esseintes calling out for some kind of connection to her? In his manipulated, artificial delights do we not perceive a recognition that no direct experience of nature is possible? (Nor direct experience of anything else, for that matter). Nature is an artificial entity, a constructed phenomenon, existing in the hearts and brains of human beings. And here, does not des Esseintes anticipate Jung's idea that everything that exists, exists first in psychic reality? Or, in more modern vein, is not *Against Nature* an anticipation of the virtual reality of the computer game and of a screen-bound, theme park culture? Nature can be *improved on* by means of culture.

Like Margaret Atwood, Huysmans cannot resist the move (almost a "natural" move, it seems) from an engagement with nature to an engagement with the social—though, for Huysmans, artifice serves as the essential mediator. What could be more *engagé*, not to say *enragé*, than these lines from *Against Nature*?

> Under the pretext of encouraging liberty and progress, society has discovered yet another means of aggravating man's wretched lot, by dragging him from his home, rigging him out in a ridiculous costume, putting specially designed weapons into his hands, and reducing him to the same degrading slavery from which the negroes were released out of pity—and all this to put him in a position to kill his neighbour without risking the scaffold, as ordinary murderers do who operate single-handed, without uniforms, and with quieter, poorer weapons. (Huysmans, 1884, pp. 196–197)

But Huysmans wouldn't be Huysmans and des Esseintes wouldn't be des Esseintes if these anti-war sentiments were not immediately followed by this remarkable *non sequitur*:

> Ah! If in the name of pity the futile business of procreation was ever to be abolished, the time had surely come to do it. (Huysmans, 1884, p. 197)

Flexible specialisation

Viewed imaginatively, des Esseintes stands as a kind of economic and technological pioneer rather than an omnipotent narcissistic type seeking to control nature. His work is carried out at home, not in office, factory, or field. He makes constant use of technology—the mouth organ, the perfume-making apparatus, the room on gimbals, the syringe for rectal feeding. Following trends in development economics, des Esseintes uses technology that can be characterised as "appropriate technology", operating on a small scale and with regard to environmental and social costs (see Kaplinsky, 1990). From the standpoint of the 1990s, it was hard at first to share des Esseintes's enthusiasm for technology, yet, in spite of ecologistic alterations in cultural consciousness, we in the West remain committed to and dependent on technology. Technology is, for us, a part of nature. Des Esseintes seems to know just which technology or, more accurately, which level of technology to apply to his consciously chosen tasks. In this sense, he can act as an imaginal bridge between a perspective that would restrict appropriate (or intermediate) technology to developing countries and one that could sense that the same pragmatic, modest approach might have applicability in the industrially advanced countries.

Another concept, also taken from development economics, which finds symbolisation in des Esseintes's activities, and even in his personality, is that of "flexible specialisation" (Hoffman & Kaplinsky, 1988). When I first heard this term, I thought immediately of human psychology because the capacity to perform many separate tasks according to the quite specific dictates of consciousness is characteristic of our species. In fact, the theories of flexible specialisation are a response to the limitations of models of industrialism founded on mass production. In mass production, purpose-built machines are used by semi-skilled workers to produce standardised products. Standardisation of the product permits economies of scale and helps to maximise profits. Flexible specialisation, on the other hand, requires a combination of craft skill and flexible equipment—maybe electronics-based machinery that can be reprogrammed. As Hoffman and Kaplinsky put it, we are (and, I would add in 2015, still are) at a transitional point between the eras of "machinofacture" and "systemofacture" (pp. 64–69). It may be that we are entering an era of technological Darwinism. It is important, for the developing countries *and* the industrially advanced countries, that flexible specialisation kill off mass production because flexible specialisation could then come into its own as the globally appropriate approach to technology for this new century.

That it should happen is important when we consider the possibility that environmentally linked conflicts may well erupt in the developing world in the near future—for example, conflicts over scarce supplies of water or large-scale migrations caused by desertification. The Gulf War of 1991 may also have been a precursor of other resource wars.

However, none of this will mean anything, and we run the risk of staying on a des Esseintes level of practicality, if we do not address the contemporary form of slavery represented by international debt. Developing economies need emancipating from the burden of debt and this will be facilitated by changes in mindset in the industrially advanced countries. The debts of the Third World were not incurred—are not being incurred—under a system of rules of fair play. Flexible specialisation and appropriate technology may produce export-led growth, but the foreign currency never reaches the producers. If we consider a development problem such as the feminisation of poverty, the trend in which women's economic lot often worsens as the wealth of their community increases, then the disaster that is going on right now is a deathly disaster for women and children (see Goldberg & Kren, 1991; Sen, 1989). The human rights of women and children are integral to effective and sustainable development. People have some "right to development", no matter how artificial or against nature that turns out to be. Even the arch-dandy, aesthete of aesthetes, hyper-misogynist Duc Jean Floressas des Esseintes would agree (at least I think he would).

Links

Let me review some of the links between *Surfacing* and *Against Nature*. There is a searching examination in both novels of the relations between culture and nature, leading to all manner of destabilisations of our habitual diagrams of these relations. Second, in both novels the protagonists explore the possibility of a transcendence of the body. Third, there is in both novels an explicit search, by means of excess, whether natural excess or artificial excess, for a more fruitful relation to nature. As far as I can tell from empathic identification with both writers, the result should not interfere with the fullest possible living out of an unbalanced, supposedly one-sided position: "I am a place", says Atwood's narrator (Atwood, 1972a, p. 109); "But I just don't enjoy the pleasures other people enjoy", says des Esseintes (Huysmans, 1884, p. 34). Fourth and last, both writers are concerned with the relation between depth and the surface, the particular depth to be found on the surface, when surfacing; the unnatural depth of the environment.

What I have been trying to do is to construct a spectrum of responses to environmentalism out of the narratives, imageries, and underlying ethoses of the two novels *Surfacing* and *Against Nature*. What happens if we allow Atwood's narrator and des Esseintes to have a baby? What if des Esseintes were the father instead of Joe? What would *that* baby be like?

Environmentalism, ecopsychology, and education

Unlike Margaret Atwood, I have had to combine in one chapter imaginative, fantasy thinking and pragmatic, directed thinking. What follows is both a depth psychological contribution to the many debates about environmentalism and an attempt to answer the question with which I ended the previous section: What *would* the baby look like?

The ideogram that is born out of this joint presentation of fantasy thinking and pragmatic thinking is that of *change*. Maybe the image of change always underpinned my argument already. One message of the environmental movement has been that we must change the way that we live and this will have to be done on the basis of changes in the ways we apprehend our relation to nature. It is hard to say succinctly whether the environmental movement is truly for or secretly against change. In the sense that environmentalism represents an opposition to the forms of social organisation established in the industrially advanced countries in the past two centuries, the environmental movement supports a change. But in the sense that environmentalists, along with everyone else, have not caught up in consciousness with the techno-industrial revolutions of the past two hundred years, and are rooted in a pre-industrial cultural matrix, environmentalism may be seen as being against the very changes that have already happened. Hence, environmentalism may be regarded as deeply conservative.

But the key question, in all its school debating society naivety, remains: Does, or can, human nature change? We saw how Atwood developed the eternal to point up the mutable. Des Esseintes does artificially what comes to us naturally by creating a new microculture. Oscar

Wilde, profoundly influenced by Huysmans, wrote in his tract "The soul of man under socialism" that "The only thing we know about human nature is that it changes. Change is the one quality we can predict of it. ... The systems that fail are those that rely on the permanency of human nature, and not on its growth and development" (1978, p. 1010).

I think that what our thinking and feeling lacks most is a unit—I mean a unit of size and space—which is a comfortable one to have in mind when discussing environmental concerns. The temptation is to propose the world itself (as in the Gaia theory) or, at the other extreme, to focus on the bottle bank in one's own neighbourhood. We are, after all, embarking on nothing less than an exploration of the psychology of the earth, of what in Britain is called soil and Americans call dirt. How does the very ground on which you stand, on which you grew up, contribute to who you are?

Not a conclusion

There can be no conclusion to a chapter such as this one. I am aware of its dissonances and jerkiness. The making of pragmatic suggestions when confronted with insoluble problems is itself an act of faith; there is an undecidability that cannot be denied. So the move on which I want to end is to salute the conception, or rather the construction, of a new kind of actor, an environmental actor with an environmentally attuned political consciousness. Atwood's words from the closing passage of *Surfacing* chime with this:

> I bring with me from the distant past five nights ago the time-traveller, the primaeval one who will have to learn, shape of a gold-fish now in my belly, undergoing its watery changes. Word furrows potential in its proto-brain, untravelled paths. No god and perhaps not real, even that is uncertain; I can't know yet, it's too early. (Atwood, 1972a, p. 187)

Or, in des Esseintes's words, at the end of a meditation on the evil triviality of the power held by the bourgeoisie whose only interest is the accumulation of wealth:

> Well, crumble then, society! Perish, old world! (Huysmans, 1884, p. 199)

Both des Esseintes and the heroine of *Surfacing* are responding to the pressures of their time and place in a highly individual manner. This is the license of the fictional! But for ordinary citizens, the question of the significance or lack of it in an individual contribution to cultural and political struggle and change is a massive open question, which I try to address in the next chapter on whether or not any one individual can "make a difference", as so many desire to do. This matter of "making a difference" in the political world comes up in my therapy practice over and over, and I think that, from the success of the phenomenon of online generated letter-writing campaigns and signing petitions, the question of "what's a poor boy [or girl] gonna do" remains as mind-scrambling as ever.

CHAPTER FIVE

Making a difference—what can an individual do?

When presenting this material in lecture or workshop format, I begin by playing Ennio Morricone's theme music from the 1966 spaghetti western *The Good, the Bad and the Ugly* (Leone, 1966). The Man with No Name, the Clint Eastwood character, is the consummate individual: he needs no name. Readers with access to the internet could perhaps go now to YouTube to listen (again?) to the music: http://www.youtube.com/watch?v = LQGGQ-FCe_w

The direct and interactive approach of this chapter is also maintained by a series of experiential exercises. I am sure that this article could only have been written by a man in his sixties, enabled by time and its ravages to be less cautious and correct. The music is also a bit of self-mockery: ironic and, I hope, suggestive.

It may seem perverse to call for a return to the notion of the individual in progressive political theorising at a time when so many bemoan the collapse of social and communal ties in Western societies. Families don't go bowling any more—and you (the author) want *more* individualism when everyone is already looking after "Number One", in an ethos of *sauve qui peut*?

I hope I may appear less weird if I say that, in a nutshell, I am wondering if there is a place still in radical politics for individualism and the idea of the individual. My enquiry is into whether or not there can be a theoretical back-up to ideas of "making a difference" via individual entry into political activism. This is a rather emotive topic as I have encountered it in the clinical situation and in workshops under the general rubric of "political clinics". Citizens may want to make a difference, and they know that, in order to do so, they must join with other like-minded citizens. In which case, what will become of their individuality? Even actively engaging in political activism cannot really silence doubts about the limits of personal responsibility. Then there are questions of impact and efficacy. Clients speak about these themes, ruefully and sometimes cynically: everything seems so "massive", so "wrong", so "unchanging". I confess that it was very hard to write this chapter. It came from an inner place, and is quite contrary to what I usually think in my roles as political consultant, activist, and academic. In those situations, how many times have I explained that there is no such thing as an individual and that individuals are socially constructed, even when they believe themselves to be autonomous and inner directed entities?

I still think the political world and the social class that an individual inhabits are vitally important. We need also to move beyond the social and the human to consider what is being developed in terms of eco-psychology and eco-criticism (Rust & Totton, 2012)—but it is the *experience* of being an individual that interests me at the moment, no matter how illusory that might be on an intellectual plane. Here, much of the contemporary sociological project on the rise of a self-invented identity, cut off from traditional contexts, strikes me as experience—distant, notwithstanding the many ways in which it is challenging and useful. As Layton (2013) has shown, sociologists today, such as Giddens (1991) or Beck and Beck-Gernsheim (2002), have reached the conclusion that the individual needs to be better theorised, though this is usually in order to make a deeper and more fecund contribution to their own discipline of sociology. Nevertheless, the realisation that subjectivity and the individual need to be understood with reference to the social sciences chimes with my project.

Crucially, Layton (2013) has explained how ideas about individuals, collectives, culture, contexts, and constructions have themselves got a particular history and are themselves subject to the relativising they propose for individuals. Reading some of this literature, it has occurred to me that the "sociological individual" of the past twenty-five years could be summarised as being interested mainly in her or his life and issues, and not in the life of the times and its issues. As Layton put it:

> Rose (1989), for example, has critiqued the work of Giddens and Beck, arguing that "individualization" has not just been about the expansion of autonomy to an ever-widening portion of the population, but rather has been about the creation and extension of a certain version of subjectivity and autonomy. (Layton, 2013, p. 139)

The problem I am addressing is that the sociologically perceived narcissism and plasticity of that kind of individual actually depotentiate her or him as far as political activism is concerned. I am sure that this is not deliberate but, rather, inadvertent. Hence, in a fresh effort to bridge the gap between the self-invented individual and his or her entry into political activism and engagement, I introduce later in the chapter some material about "political types", showing how political activity itself may be explored from an individualistic perspective. The hope is that this kind of contribution will lead to a reconfiguration of "individual" and "collective" or "social". Then we might be in a position to revisit in contemporary terms the notion of "organic" solidarity in a society as opposed to "mechanical" solidarity, to use Durkheim's (1893) words.

Beyond context

In academic discourse—and also in politics, whether mainstream, progressive or reactionary—the idea of the individual *tout seul* simply does not pass muster these days. Context and construction are all: family, group, community, society, culture, nation. This contemporary discourse stresses that individuals are embedded and constructed by and in social relationships, communal networks, task-oriented groups, and ecosystems. This isn't wrong, of course, but has the potential of an individual to contribute actively to what happens in the collective been underestimated by this set of assumptions? Is there an overreaction in which the desire to be intellectually correct has meant that we now refer to contexts within which individuals exist—but not to those individuals themselves?

Amongst the psychoanalytic writers who most vividly foregrounded the question of the relations between the individual and the collective was Carl Jung (1875–1961). His writings are peppered with iterations of this question. My proposal is that, if Jungian psychology could somehow refashion its approach to the individual, then it could become a source of support and inspiration to embattled citizens whose experience of their battles is often that they are in it on their own. Jung was one of the first to explain that "there is a human desire to 'belong', to conform, to relinquish individual responsibility and find a king, a dictator, a boss who will tell you what to do" (Helena Bassil-Morozow, personal communication, July 2012).

> Exercise: We can all think of individuals who have "made a difference". Sometimes, you may feel you have yourself made a difference. Think of times when you personally as an individual have made a difference in some situation or other, whether an important situation or something relatively less important. What happened?

Has the academy gone too far in stressing the contingent and context-bound nature of an individual person? Are the professors saying "There's no such thing as an individual"? What does it mean that Cushman (1995) titled a book *Constructing the Self, Constructing America*? Is the consensus that the idea of individuals is just another bit of constructivism? Is Levinas right, with his ethical stress on alterity, on the other, on someone other than the individual (Levinas, 1995)? I think it is important to explore these questions because many of the horrid conformist features of contemporary Western societies rest on the idea that "you belong". This easily becomes "you *should* belong", and then slips into some variant of "you belong to *us*". Society does its bit to get us all to stay in context—even the bankers! Joining the system is more or less compulsory.

The opposites of constructionism and contextualism are essentialism, universality, and eternity. As some Jungian commentators, including myself (Samuels, 1993) have noted, these can lead to a kind of "archetypal determinism", which, in its own way, can be massively damaging to the idea of the individual whom Jung said he valued so much.

Here's a bit of self-criticism. I have written about and conducted a workshop exercise called "Where did you get your politics from?" We look at parents, family, ethnicity, class, nationality, and all imaginable other influences, but what about the accidental, or even the constitutional factor, the *individual* factor: some ineluctable and irreducible piece of chance or fate that enters into the realm of political choices and actions, something that cannot be explained by context? Just thinking about what we could call "political style" or "political type" enables us to recuperate the idea of the individual with regard to social responsibility. I come back to this question of political type later.

Anyway, the conventional wisdom is that we are always in groups, networks, contexts. By now this may have become banal and, without critique, destructive. Where has the individual gone in progressive discourse? In the spoken version of this chapter, I sang as follows, to the tune of "Where have all the flowers gone?" (Seeger, 1955):

> Where have all the individuals gone, long time passing?
> Where have all the individuals gone, long time ago?
> Where have all the individuals gone? Professors have banned
> them every one.
> Oh, when will they ever learn?
> Oh, when will they ever learn?

Of course, economic and ethnic factors inform "subjectivity". Of course, we are relational beings, and it is important to assert that we are not atomised, split-up entities sitting in empty space, but the shadow aspect of this is that it plays into the ever-increasing centralisation of society. British readers will assuredly not have been fooled by the fantasy of involvement in "the Big Society", the flagship policy of the 2010 UK Conservative Party general election campaign, which then formed part of the legislative programme of the Conservative-Liberal Democrat Coalition Agreement, which aimed to create a climate that empowers local people and communities, building a "big society" that takes power away from politicians and gives it to the people. Rather, it's all about central control; individuals are coerced into neighbourhood groups and societies: join or die! Your society needs you!

All of this adherence to "the context" is the Zeitgeist for the industrialisation of psychotherapy that is going on in many countries: they want to legislate, regulate, manualise, and standardise us; they want to get the power to decide which individuals are "fit to practise" and which are not. Even the clinical encounter itself seems to exclude individuals. Everyone is "relational" nowadays. "It's the relationship, stupid!" was seriously proposed as the banner headline for a campaign in favour of the "talking therapies". Again, it's not my experience that the clinical encounter really excludes individuals; it's the discourses on the clinical that sometimes seem to do so.

Relational intersubjectivity may undermine or exclude individual subjectivity. It's "the therapeutic relationship" that is supposed to take the strain, not the sweating individuals who compose it. It's all about dyads, dialogue, communication, attachment, attunement, rupture and repair, transference-countertransference. This refusal of one-person psychology has gone too far. The therapeutic relationship has become an oppressive, conventional, moralistic norm (see Samuels, 2014).

I hope my argument becomes clearer: it is that the shadow of understanding ourselves as group beings in contexts is that we unwittingly support many of the things we hate. We norm, we conform, but we very rarely storm.

Solidarity becomes a curse as well as a blessing, a cul-de-sac, not the way ahead. Although I am a supporter of ecopsychology, I think this shadow groupishness and enforced belonging stalks many ecosystemic approaches to politics. Where's the individual when the discourse is planetary? Can the Earth really be so hostile to the individual?

Let's explore the old liberal idea of the individual, the individual subject, and root it in a new critical anti-relational discourse. Let's see if we can refresh our idea of political action by engaging with the individual and individualism a bit. Classical individualism stresses the moral worth of the individual who is its focus. The fundamental premise is that the human individual is of primary importance in the struggle for liberation. Individualism is thus also associated with artistic and bohemian interests and lifestyles: self-creation and experimentation as opposed to tradition or mass opinion. This is what analysis and psychotherapy used to be before they got bourgeoisified and subjected to *déformation professionnelle*.

I'd like to suggest that we can revise this monolithic and overly solid approach quite a bit to take in the idea of the individual as fractured. The fact that an individual is fractured is not an obstacle to radical politics; rather it is a source of them. The individual is a bridge: between the inner and outer, between the personal and the political, between introverted solitude and being in a network; an individual who is more of an uprooted anti-hero than a hero: a bum, a schlemiel, a nomad. Someone who *feels* "self-begotten", just as Milton's (1667) Satan said he was, *pace* the psychoanalytic strictures against "parthenogenetic delusion", never mind the ablation of God. Why not be inflated? Has there ever been a successful revolutionary who was not necessarily, gloriously, and insanely inflated?

Clearly, there is more to psychology than the isolated individual human being and much has been usefully done to get rid of that idea, but academics have set up a false situation here. If we simplistically equate the idea of the individual with the conscious ego, or with sentimental Jungian, romantic ahistorical trumpeting of the supremacy of the individual, then hurrah for the intellectuals who've got rid of a dangerously misleading conception! This unthinking and reactionary version, however, is not the only possible playing out of the individual.

The individual who needs our attention today has never been like that, has never been solely the product of puritanism, nor snow-white, nor a romantic cliché, nor the unified being of orthodox psychology, nor Freudian ego, nor Jungian Self, nor a humanistic ideal. Do those pristine creatures, who would certainly deserve critique, really exist? No. I suggest that the individual who stalks contemporary culture, and who is trying to return to its politics, has *always* been a decentred subject, an actor performing many roles in many scripts, characterised by lack, somewhat faded as well as jaded: jerky, marginalised, alienated, split, guilty, empty, imaginary. The individual has *always* been a Trickster in his or her practice of politics.

I think there is something we can do with this de-idealised, putrefied, violent, and marvellously rebellious individual. The internally pluralistic individual is the *means* to an engagement with politics and culture, not an *obstacle* to it.

Make no mistake, as I mentioned earlier, individuals in the West are today in agony. It is an agony that politics is so broken. It is also an agony how political language has collapsed. George Orwell was prescient in his novel *1984* (Orwell, 1949) when he tells us that Ingsoc and the Thought Police had a project to *reduce* the size of the dictionary, hence banishing the nuanced conversation needed for intimate and political life alike.

In both clinical work with clients and in political clinics (workshops open to the public), I've found that individual bodies bear this agony just as much as individual minds and psyche—*agon* means to writhe. In a sense, today's body is more than ever a writhing body politic, and is always armoured against attack or loss; people cannot breathe because of pollution; there's a constant state of adrenalisation; consumerist pressures tyrannise us into thinking we are either too fat or too thin; and we are obsessed with medications that we know will fail us.

Recuperating the Jungian individual

Those of a Jungian persuasion may be smugly thinking that this argument is preaching to the choir. Such critics would be thinking that they already have a coherent theory of the individual firmly in place, for Jung is well known for having linked the idea of personal individuation and collective phenomena (Jung, 1953, para. 267). I have to say that I am not convinced.

Be that as it may, when Jung wrote about "the individual", academics turn away and snigger. The Jungian individual doesn't cut the intellectual—or political—mustard. The way in which Jung positioned the individual in relation to society, and the way in which society is reduced to "the mass" or "the masses", simply assumes that societies and individuals are inevitably antipathetic. Never mind that, at times, Jung seemed to suggest that a society or a nation is simply made up of the individuals in it, and there is nothing more to be said. In 1956, Jung wrote of:

> the agglomeration of huge masses in which the individual disappears anyway ... the individual [is robbed] of his [sic] foundations and his dignity. As a social unit he has lost his individuality and becomes a mere abstract number in the bureau of statistics, He can only play the role of an interchangeable unit of infinitesimal importance. (Jung, 1957, para 501)

It's hardly surprising then, that he continues in sardonic, sceptical, and depressive vein:

> Looked at rationally and from outside, that is exactly what he is, and from this point of view it seems positively absurd to go on talking about the value or meaning of the individual. Indeed, one can hardly imagine how one ever came to endow human life with so much dignity when the truth to the contrary is as plain as the palm of your hand. (Jung, 1957, para 501)

I think that this sense of the impossibility of the individual in relation to society represents a premature concession by Jung; it is just too pessimistic and melancholic, though the rhetoric is splendid: "an interchangeable unit of infinitesimal importance".

Can we recuperate the Jungian idea of the individual? To do so would involve critiquing the relationship between individual and society as Jung set it out. In a recent discussion, David Tacey (2012) succinctly summarised Jung from his book *The Undiscovered Self* (Jung, 1957) as making "a romantic defence of individuality and a warning against collectivism—[but] it makes for an odd kind of sociology if Jung sees the social mass only as something that wants to swallow the individual".

Commenting on the draft doctoral manuscript that eventually became Ira Progoff's (1952) *Jung's Psychology and Its Social Meaning*, Jung 1952) said: "the individual in society may be understood as a piece of the archetype ... The archetype of the individual is the Self. The Self is all embracing" (p. 216). Tacey is correct: it is an odd approach to the social.

The way I see it, in *The Undiscovered Self*, Jung also got a lot of it right, and specifically the way in which the individual is ruined and controlled by the state: "[I]t is small wonder that individual judgement grows increasingly uncertain of itself and that *responsibility is collectivised as much as possible, i.e., is shuffled off by the individual and delegated to a corporate body*" (Jung, 1957, para 504, emphasis added).

Unfortunately, there is more than Jung's "odd sociology" to hold back the evolving of links between his ideas and a progressive, humane politics. Jung's ideas on the individual are aristocratic, elitist, and supercilious. I am thinking here about his awful reference to "stunted individuals":

> It is obvious that a social group consisting of stunted individuals cannot be a healthy and viable institution; only a society that can preserve its internal cohesion and collective values, while at the same time granting the individual the greatest possible freedom, has any prospect of enduring vitality. As the individual is not just a single, separate being, but by his very existence presupposes a collective relationship, it follows that the process of individuation must lead to more intense and broader collective relationships and not to isolation. (Jung, 1921, para 758)

I want to go head to head with Jung here: "Look, CG, the stunted individual is the only bloody individual that there is. Just as you taught us about alchemy, we begin political struggle with base materials: citizens who are far from individuated, who inhabit a world you've told us does not want them to individuate."

Similarly, from his paper on "Adaptation, individuation, collectivity" (Jung, 1916): "Whoever is not creative enough [to individuate] must re-establish collective conformity with a group of his own choice, otherwise he remains an empty waster and windbag" (para. 1098). So we have stunted individuals here, wasters and windbags over there, and truly individuated people in the first-class cabin. No wonder Sonu Shamdasani (2003) summarised Jung as saying "individuation was for the few" (p. 307), but there are a lot of people in the world, not just "the few", and not just the Jungian 0.1 per cent.

Here Jung is like Marx, that is, the Marx who considered that the lowest of the low, the *lumpenproletariat*, were incapable of making a revolution. We should join the liberation theologians in their challenge to this Marxian elitism. For Boff (1988) it is the poorest, most downtrodden, most out-of-it who will make the revolution: "God is in the poor who cry out. And God is the one who listens to the cry and liberates, so that the poor no longer need to cry out" (p. 166). Orwell (1949) got it too: "If there is hope, it lies in the proles" (p. 89), as did the Psalmist: "The stone that the builders rejected has now become the cornerstone of the Temple" (Psalms, 118: 22).

Rebels and individuals

To this point, I have discussed whether contextualism and constructivism have gone too far; then considered the "fractured" and "stunted" individual; and considered the advantages and disadvantages of Jung's conception of the individual for a progressive politics.

I now turn to Albert Camus and his working out of the intricate connections between existence, oppression, freedom, action—and the individual. I draw for the most part on Camus's (1951) *The Rebel*, a book I first read at school, aged sixteen, and used as a base for numerous attempts to get out of my cage; *plus ça change* …

Camus stated succinctly that rebellion and revolt are critically important to the making of meaning and hence to what we could call the birth of an individual. He reaches no conclusions about the purpose and meaning of life. He is relentlessly sceptical. Hence his position is that there is a fundamental absurdity to life and that attempts to create meaning, which are innate and valuable, are also—crucially—attempts to avoid the unavoidable absurdity of existence. Here Camus's twinning of despair and a kind of ironic hope reminds us of Beckett, but he is also, suggestively, very like Jung, as this quote from *The Red Book* shows: "Meaning is a moment and a transition from absurdity to absurdity, and absurdity only a moment and a transition from meaning to meaning" (Jung, 2009, p. 242).

The Rebel is a history of humanity in revolt. Over time, humans have displayed a basic rejection of injustice; hence they rebel. All one can believe in is the value of protest and the protester's life. Crucially, for Camus (1951), the impulse to rebel is inborn! "To breathe is to judge" (p. 8). The act of rebellion is a primary given of human life. Revolt creates dignity and the ethical life—and solidarity. Individuals who rebel against oppressive state are transformed into a collective force: "*I rebel, therefore we are*" (ibid., p. 111; original emphasis). The rebellious individual is the progenitor of the social movement.

Now, if the impulse to rebel is inborn and hence archetypal, then any idea that Jung and Camus are total opposites may not be the case. Camus's default position is that human nature is made by decisions and acts, whereas Jung's conception of human nature is different—but Jung is not only about archetypal determinism either. Remember: "Confrontation with an archetype or instinct is an *ethical* problem of the first magnitude" (Jung, 1947, para 410, emphasis in original) and there are many references to "free will" throughout Jung's *Collected Works*.

I find Jung and Camus as writers rather similar: neither is rational or linear; both use metaphor, and are interested in psychological experience; both write in the face of the catastrophes of the twentieth century. Camus, however, rejects the collective as a given; for him, rebellion creates whatever is more-than-personal.

What I take from Camus for this discussion on "the individual" is that, while the original motivation to rebel may be inborn and individual, it becomes buried because of social and other repressions. Political individuality arises from rebellion which then may lead to joining others in solidarity. Camus admitted that people have a longing for something *social*, but also in the *spiritual* area. He called it "religion" or "philosophy" (Camus, 1951, p. 237), but I think it is more accurately termed "social spirituality".

In social spirituality, individuals come together to take action in the social sphere, doing this in concert with other people. When this happens, something spiritual comes into being. Being actively engaged in a social, political, cultural, or ethical issue, together with others, initiates the spiritual. This is a very different perspective from one that would see social spirituality as being something done in the social domain by spiritual, that is, individuated, people. On the contrary, there is a kind of spiritual rain that can descend on ordinary individuals who get involved in politics and social issues with others, and hence "social" spirituality (see Samuels, 2001).

The difference from Jung's elitist conception of the individual should be clear: this is by no means an elitist perspective. Social spirituality embraces people who get involved with other people in political and social action: for example, the Occupy movement or the protests against global capitalism that young people are into. What they're doing when they get involved in the anti-capitalist movements and the environmental and ecological movements is to participate in a general resacralisation of culture (Samuels, 1993). To play on the word "politicised", many of them are becoming "spiritualised". When one gets involved in idealistic politics, sometimes, not always, one gets spiritualised, and so the anti-capitalist movement is creating its own spirituality and, in turn, is being informed by the spirituality that it creates. Political action leads to spirituality of some kind and spirituality informs political action. Of course, eventually it all falls to pieces: either the police wreck it or people (allegedly) "grow up", but there is a basic resacralising tendency worth recognising. But, as I said, you cannot guarantee that it will all be left-wing.

Exercise: Think of times you feel someone or something was trying to prevent you from being an individual—family, society, peer pressure, shame, whatever. Did you rebel—or not? In either case, what happened?

Individual political types

Now, as promised, I introduce a frankly individual and experiential element into the discussion. I mentioned that there are questions of individual political *style* or political *type* to consider.

What follows was first fashioned out of working with a mixed group of Israeli Palestinians and Israelis Jews in Jerusalem in the early 1990s. It became clear that, aside from the obvious irreconcilable differences in how the Middle East political scene was understood, there were individuals on both sides of the divide who were participating in the group in very similar or identical ways. I pointed this out and divided the larger group differently along style and type lines rather than content lines. I put the warlike with the warlike, the historically minded with the historically minded, the diplomatic with the diplomatic, the visionaries with the visionaries. The basic disagreements were there but the participants were now in groups with others whose political type or style resembled their own. There were discernible improvements in comprehension and even in goodwill.

The warring factions were presented not with an analysis of what they were saying (that came later), but with a panorama of the ways in which they were saying it, that is to say, with the style or type of politics they were using—for "It ain't what you *say* but the *way* that you say it … that's what gets results."

So the various people in conflict are operating in very different political styles or types. My inspiration for this was, in general terms, Jung's model of psychological types: extraversion, introversion, thinking, feeling, sensation, intuition. As in life generally, for a variety of reasons, some of them to do with their personal backgrounds, some to do with their inborn political constitutions, people will live out the political aspects of their lives in different ways. Over time, I've developed a list of images of differing political types as follows, in a spectrum ranging from active styles to passive ones: *warrior, terrorist, exhibitionist, leader, activist, parent, follower, child, martyr, victim, trickster, healer, analyst, negotiator, bridge-builder, diplomat, philosopher, mystic, ostrich.*

Some individuals will be violent terrorists; some pacifists. Some will want empirical back-up for their ideas; others will fly by the seat of their pants. Some will definitely enjoy co-operative political activity; others will suffer the nightmare of trying to accomplish things in a group only because they passionately believe in the ends being pursued. Let's not make the mistake of insisting that everyone do it in precisely the same way. If we are to promote political creativity, we need to value and honour individual political styles and types, and to think of ways of protecting such diversity.

As described, the notion of political type is particularly useful when addressing conflict, whether interpersonal or within organisations or even between nations or between parts of nations. Just as introverts and extraverts suffer from mutual incomprehension, individuals or groups that employ a particular political type often have very little idea about how the other person or group is actually "doing" their politics. This is not to say that political content per se is irrelevant, only that there may be more that divides opponents than their different views. When working on questions of political type, it isn't necessary to encourage anyone to stick to just one type. In fact, the opposite holds true. Some individuals will use one political style in one setting and quite another in a different one. A negotiator at work may be a terrorist at home, or people may have, to borrow Jung's words, a "superior" political type, an "inferior" political type, and "auxiliary" styles; thus a warrior may have neglected his philosopher, or a diplomat his activist.

The idea is to become comfortable with as vast a range of political types as possible. Jung said that individuation involved activating all the types, and both extraversion and introversion.

Exercise: Reflecting on the political types, (a) choose the one you do the best/more often; (b) choose the one you are poor or ineffective at and might work on in order to develop; and (c) reflect on whether there are any you cannot imagine using.

The limits of individual responsibility

It is now time to probe the limits of individual responsibility—to think about not making a difference.

What, then, is the scope of our individual responsibility for others and for the world? The roots of the word "responsibility" lie in *spondere*, to promise or pledge, but what happens if we promise too much? In politics—and, I suppose, in life—there is a problem of people being too demanding of themselves. If we cannot live up to these demands, our idealism and energy go underground and are self-supressed. We seem politically apathetic but, secretly, we are not: secretly, we are in touch with our "inner politician".

Let us think about how this banishing of political energy and ideal-ism affects *tikkun olam*—Hebrew for the repair and restoration of the world. We are back to the problem of "the stunted individual". If one tries to do *tikkun* from too perfect a self-state, it won't work because the only possible way to approach and engage with a broken and frac-tured world of which one is a part is, surely, as a broken and fractured, stunted individual: an individual with death in mind.

I call the broken and fractured one the "good-enough individual", once again using Winnicott's epithet out of context, but again not overlooking his interest in how the parent helps the baby to steer a path between idealisation and denigration of the parent.

Here, we are talking of the individual's own path between self-idealisation and self-denigration. Winnicott (1951) said that "as time proceeds [the mother] adapts less and less completely, gradually, according to the infant's growing ability to deal with her failure" (p. 238). We can gloss this to say that, inevitably, an individual will fail himself or herself—but this failure can be done in the individual's own way. Hence, failure to make a difference in the world to the extent one hopes becomes much less shameful, one becomes less self-denigrating. It becomes okay to fail. This is important because shame at failure is what leads to depression and guilt and so destroys the impulse and the capacity for action.

Individuals need a different attitude to their failure, particularly the failure of their political hopes and aspirations and projects. Here's a selection:

- "Failure is the key to the kingdom within" (Rumi, 2006)
- "[E]very attempt is a wholly new start, and a different kind of failure" (Eliot, 1943)
- "Fail again. Fail better" (Beckett, 1983)
- "[T]here's no success like failure/And … failure's no success at all" (Dylan, 1965).

Perhaps this is the kind of thing Camus meant when he wrote that:

> The rebel can never find peace. He knows what is good, and despite himself, does evil. The value which supports him is never given to him once and for all—he must fight to support it, unceasingly. (1951, p. 206)

Exercise: Think of times when you yourself made a difference and also of times when you wanted to but failed in the attempt.

Before we pack up in despair and go home, let us once again recall that the official politicians and the governments of the world, with all possible resources at their disposal, have not done such a terrific job of managing things. Governments constantly try to improve things in the political world, usually by redistributing wealth or changing legislative and constitutional structures or defusing warlike situations. But to achieve real change, we may have to turn to "the man with no name".

CHAPTER SIX

Promiscuities: politics, psychology, imagination, and spirituality (and a note on hypocrisy)

Background

An opportunity to speak at a conference to mark the fortieth anniversary of May 1968 enabled some of us who were around then to reflect on the personal and political trajectories of our lives and to discuss it all with younger colleagues. I chose to present on "Promiscuity—then and now" and used the moment to work up reflections on sexuality and social critique in a historical framework. The responses the presentation evoked were highly charged as memories, many of them doubtless held in the body, played into the current positions and preoccupations of the audience.

In 1968 I had just dropped out of Oxford. The year before, Jefferson Airplane told us "You better find somebody to love". There was a revolution supposed to be going on and no one would need degrees in the society that would emerge. As part of involvement in anti-apartheid politics, I had been briefly imprisoned in South Africa and beaten up, so the student movement seemed a really safe place to be. My main interest was in politically engaged experimental theatre and members of the company I founded (the Oxford Progressive Theatre Group) lived communally and engaged in considered and considerable sexual experimentation. There were joys to this but also a good deal of pain as jealousy, arising out of the very training for monogamy we were contesting, was rife. At the time, such experimentation was almost an ideological requirement.

I moved into youth work with "unclubbable" teenagers, still using drama. Here, I encountered equally non-traditional sexual behaviours but apparently devoid of ideology. I still reflect on the class divide wherein youthful Oxford dropouts behaved sexually in much the same way as disadvantaged kids in an impoverished South Wales new town—but the associations and cultural referents could not have been more different.

Then I slipped into encounter groups, psychiatric social work, and Jungian analysis. I started analytical training in 1974 and qualified in 1977. Hence I fit the story told by the psychotherapist organisers of the conference: "many radicals found their way into psychotherapy trainings". The story is a bit more complicated than this. Some radicals stayed radical even as therapists. After all, there were in the 1970s several politically progressive therapy projects such as Red Therapy and the Women's Therapy Centre that demonstrated the viability of a hybrid organisation. But some radicals took a much more conservative and Establishment direction in terms of psychotherapy.

I am one of those who became devoted to the idea that there could be a hybrid of politics and psychotherapy and this led, amongst other things, to the founding of Psychotherapists and Counsellors for Social Responsibility, Antidote (a campaign for emotional literacy in the public sphere), political consultancy with politicians and political groups, and professional work in the areas known variously as inclusivity, diversity, equal opportunities. I was active in the campaign to remove discrimination against lesbians and gay men who were seeking psychoanalytic training.

More recently, I added a third side to the coin, welcoming both the political and psychological relevance to psychotherapy of spiritual and transpersonal ideas. All may be considered "more-than-personal". In my writing, I have introduced the idea of a "resacralisation of culture" (Samuels, 1993, pp. 3–23) and developed a contemporary and progressive "anatomy of spirituality" (Samuels, 2001, pp. 122–134; 2004, pp. 201–211). I return to these ideas later.

The problem with promiscuity

In the 1960s, reference was to "non-possessive relating" or "alternative families" or "free love". No one used the word "promiscuity". I have decided to retain this word for political and intellectual as well as shock reasons. I do not want to end up merely complementing monogamy by writing about a kind of serial monogamy. For many (not all) more recent polyamorous discourses seem to assume that such relationships will be long-term (or at least not terribly short-term). I'll return to the crucial value-judgement role played by elapsed time later in the chapter but for now will indicate that I am trying to explore the implications of a divorce between sex and relationship. This is an explosive and paradox-ridden topic. At the conference, I was taken for an idiot for apparently assuming that there could be sex outside of relationship. The point was (correctly) made that any interpersonal encounter involves a relationship. Therefore my critic had made it clear that, for her, no matter how lustful and transient a physical encounter, there is a real (in the sense of implicit) relationship present. Yet, at the same time, she evinced a marked hostility to and contempt for promiscuity, which, she said, could not involve a real (in the sense of authentic) relationship. This led to some participants questioning the value-laden relational category difference "committed/uncommitted" in terms of sexual behaviours.

On reflection, I can see that the various territories mapped out under "monogamy", "non- monogamy", "polyamory", and "promiscuity" overlap and that there are frictions between them. Polyamory may seek to differentiate itself from promiscuity but from the standpoint of monogamy will not succeed. Non-monogamy includes both polyamory and promiscuity. Monogamy, as we know, often conceals a polyamory that is known to the partners or their circle but not beyond; this can be contrasted with wholly overt polyamory. And we know that promiscuity is completely reconcilable with monogamy. The two stalk each other. Each is the shadow of the other: the uxorious lust in their heart whilst libertines yearn for peace and quiet. The problem I am worrying away at may be exacerbated by the different habits of thought of psychotherapy/psychoanalysis and the social sciences. I come from a tradition that, despite the stress on listening, attunement, and accurate feedback, tends to be less impressed by what people state their position to be in survey or focus group.

I don't think we can leave it there, in a kind of fourfold parallelism: monogamy, non-monogamy, polyamory and promiscuity each being a path pointing in more or less the same direction to more or less the same ends. I see a lot of competition and bargaining between these relational tropes; in terms of both academic writing and personal experience, people want to justify the choices they have made. All relationships, regardless of composition, involve power issues and carry the potential for the abuse of power. But the inherent antagonism of monogamy often and non-monogamy is useful heuristically, performing a function of gluing together the discourse without arching over it. They are linked by their defensiveness against the other: monogamy defending a weak ego and low self-esteem, promiscuity perhaps a defence against the dangers of intimacy. Of course, the defensive properties of promiscuity are much more extensively theorised by therapists than those of monogamy and I return to this problem later in the chapter.

Another way to manage this question is to see that each of the four (that I selected) yearns to have what the others have—but can do no more than mourn and maybe rage for the lost hypothetical opportunity. I find it hard to say which of monogamy and non-monogamy is the foundational relational state that has been lost. It means that the mourning cannot be wished away by saying that, in one's life, one may have periods of monogamy and periods of non-monogamy. It isn't a logical mutual exclusiveness, but a psychological one.

Returning to the conference, I had thought there would be many presentations on sex or sexuality but there was only one mention in all the abstracts and that was a quote from Lacan that "there is no sexual ratio". It seems that, until the recent flowering of writing about polyamory and related matters (for example, Barker, 2004), there has been a collapse of ideology into psychopathology.

It is still hard to find much contemporary discussion of promiscuity in a Western context that does not take a negative line. The OED defines promiscuity as: "consisting of members or elements of different kinds massed together and without order; of mixed and disorderly composition or character. Without discrimination or method; confusedly mingled; indiscriminate. Making no distinctions. Casual, carelessly irregular." The word that appears over and over again in the context of sex is "casual". Casual sex is the term with which we are now most familiar.

If, thinking deconstructively, we look for antonyms of "casual", we get to words such as formal, deliberate, ceremonial, ritualistic. There is a history of promiscuity that is formal, deliberate, ceremonial, and ritualistic—usually in a religious or spiritual context (see Qualls-Corbett, 1987) or as part of pagan and Wiccan practice. This forms the background for my later excursion into spiritual and transpersonal promiscuous phenomena.

Let me say at this point, in anticipation of objections, that I think we should hold back from trying to clean this up by making an over precise distinction between the erotic and sexual or between fantasies and acts. That kind of precision can be spurious and defensive. Nor do I care to be undermined by being typed or smeared as advocating rather than investigating promiscuity.

> Exercise: Think of the last time you experienced lust (define it as you will). What happened? If you acted on it, what feelings did you have at the time, and now? If you didn't act on your experience of lust, what feelings did you have at the time, and now?

Promiscuity and politics

Promiscuity is the background phenomenon that since the late nineteenth century has underpinned numerous discussions that couple politics and sexuality. Conventional accounts of intimate relations praise them when they radiate constancy, longevity, and fidelity. But more radical accounts suggest that ownership and control of the other are also critically important. The best known of these was Friedrich Engels' *Origin of the Family, Private Property and the State* (1884, pp. 34–35) in which he states that the first class opposition that appears in history coincides with "the development of the antagonism between man and woman in monogamous marriage" especially in "the possessing classes".

The background formulation with which we are more familiar today is that you cannot have social change without deep personal change (for example, in the pattern of relationships and hence in the play of emotions)—and no personal change is possible if society remains the same. This point, first made explicitly by Otto Gross (1913a) nearly a hundred years ago, both anticipates and slightly differs from "the personal is political" in Gross's utopic and trans-rational forcefulness. (See Eichenbaum & Orbach 1982 for a nuanced discussion.) It was actually

Gross who coined the term "sexual revolution" (see Heuer, 2001, p. 663), stating that "smashing monogamy, and its even sicker form, polygamy, means not only the liberation of women, but still more that of man" (Gross, 1913b, col. 1142, translated by Gottfried Heuer).

Today's monogamy may be seen as chiming and co-symbolising with market economics and with implicit and explicit claims by powerful Western countries and corporations to "possess" planetary resources. Monogamy, it can be argued, is therefore implicated in a wide range of injustices—environmental, economic, and ethical. Now, this point can be made with greater or lesser passion, for monogamy certainly has its merits and cannot only be reduced to the level of political tyranny.

The corollary—that non-monogamy is correlated with sustainability, equality, and social justice—remains, perforce, untested though hugely suggestive. Ownership is a tendentious perspective on relationships and geopolitics alike; but public strategies for sustainability, such as the principle of "global commons", can be seen to co-symbolise with non-monogamy in the private sphere (see Samuels, 2001, pp. 115–126).

Notwithstanding these arguments, I think it is too easy to see the sexual as merely reflecting the power dynamics of the wider society. Sex is also a matter of power in and of itself and so, at the very least, there is a feedback loop in which sexual behaviours and the fantasies that both drive them and are produced by them have an impossible-to-quantify impact on the political. I have written of the ways in which the practice of "flipping" or "switching" in consensual submission-domination sexual behaviours could be seen as a metaphor for the capacity to be powerful in one sphere of life and much less powerful in another, to rule and to be ruled. Switchers don't get the idea from politics or the internalisation of social organisations and relations; they are not thinking first of a political way to behave sexually and then doing it. Do we have to say where switchers get the idea from outside of the sexual? Do we really know where they got it from, if "from" anywhere? Similarly, we can note switching between registers—as when the powerful businessman dons nappies during his regular Friday afternoon visit to a dominatrix. (The political variant of switching is best expressed in Michael Walzer's *Spheres of Justice*, 1983.)

If we consider, for example, the Midrashic story of Lilith we can understand the possible relations between politics and sexual behaviour a bit more fluidly. Lilith was Adam's first consort who was created from the earth at the same time as Adam. She was unwilling to give up her equality and argued with Adam over the position in which they should have intercourse—Lilith insisting on being on top. "Why should I lie beneath you," she argued, "when I am your equal since both of us were created from dust?" Adam was determined and began to rape Lilith who called out the magic name of God, rose into the air, and flew away. Eve was then created. Lilith's later career as an evil she-demon who comes secretly to men in the night, hence being responsible for nocturnal emissions, and as a murderer of newborns, culminated, after the destruction of the Temple, in a relationship with God as a sort of mistress.

My point is that this kind of material can be taken as much as an expression of the influence of the sexual on the political as the other way around. The experience people have of the sexual is also a motor of their politicality, political style and political values. Sexual experience and its associated imagery express an individual's psychological approach to political functioning (see Samuels, 1993, pp. 167–170; Samuels, 2001, pp. 47–53).

Concluding this section on promiscuity and politics, it is interesting to reflect on the micro-politics of non-monogamous relating, using this term to include promiscuity. The politics of relationality in these contexts include whether or not the agreement of members of officially recognised partners is to be sought and, if agreement is reached, what the meaning of such agreement might be. All relationships are political in this sense.

Historical considerations

Was there a "sexual revolution" in the 1960s that could be seen as a precursor to today's array of non-monogamous relational styles? This is an important background question to our discussions. Did attitudes to sex, sex education, the sexuality of women, to marriage, and to same-sex relations change in a way that was a major disjunct with what had come before? Or was it simply a technological shift, based on the pill? Perhaps it was something that affected so few people that it could not be called a "revolution". Some have suggested that the sexual revolution was simply an extension of market capitalism into the sexual area leading to the creation of a sexual marketplace occupied by sexual producers and consumers.

Nevertheless, many believe there was a sexual revolution, and base that on their experience or their observations of the behaviour of others. I think there are more interesting questions than the "was there or wasn't there?" kind. Belief that there was sexual revolution is a complicated thing to understand. It could be seen as the supreme triumph of nurture and culture over nature and the innate—or the reverse. The dominance of ego consciousness over the drives—or vice versa. Even scepticism about the sexual revolution may mean more than it seems. Perhaps there is a relief in such scepticism because then the status quo is protected. After all, Reich, one of the sources for mid-twentieth-century shifts in the sexual, became too much for Freud, as much for his sexual ideas as for his political ones. I am sure Reich was right to suggest Freud wrote *Civilization and its Discontents* (1930) specifically *contra* himself—and, let us add, as Heuer has suggested (personal communication, 2008), against Gross as well.

There is a contemporary temptation to indulge in a knee-jerk rejection of what Wilhelm Reich said in the introduction to *The Function of the Orgasm* (1927): "Psychic health depends upon ... the degree to which one can surrender to and experience the climax of excitation in the natural sexual act." What Reich (and others such as Roheim and Marcuse) were doing was to elaborate, with great ingenuity, some implications of Freud's theories of psychosexuality that supported the idea that politics and sexuality were "intimately bound together", in Fisher's (2007, p. 238) felicitous phrase. Hence, Fisher goes on, we tend to forget that, alongside his championing of sexual expressiveness, Reich (with varying degrees of support from Freud) advocated the rights of children and mothers, supporting legalised abortions and contraception.

Many sceptics adopt a reactionary approach. Family breakdown, teenage pregnancy, sexually transmitted diseases—these are held up as the inevitable and disastrous sequelae of the departure from traditional mores. But not all sceptics are so Burkean. Sheila Jeffreys' radical political lesbian point (1990) was that the so-called sexual revolution was just a further subtle oppression of women by men.

A note on non-monogamy in conventional politics and in psychoanalysis

As one who has written on political leadership (for example, in Chapter Two), I am interested in historical shifts concerning collective evaluations of promiscuous behaviour on the part of (usually male) politicians. The old assumption that, whatever goes on in the US, Europeans are far too sophisticated to care about the sexual lives of their political leaders does seem to have shifted in the twenty-first century. Even in Europe, it seems that Western political leaders must *appear* faithful to their spouses. Nothing guarantees the slippage from idealisation of a leader to denigration more than the discovery of promiscuous behaviour.

There is an interesting parallel with the history of psychoanalysis. Jung admitted to Freud that he suffered from "polygamous tendencies" and this gave the older man powerful character-assassinating ammunition. It was no surprise that, when evidence emerged that Freud had a physical relationship with his sister-in-law, the psychoanalytic establishment went into over-drive to smear the researchers. In intellectual and professional life, as in politics, it's the zipper that counts.

Promiscuity and spirituality

Having reviewed some of the problems with the idea of promiscuity, and placed my ideas in a historical context, I want further to deepen and complexify the discussion by positioning promiscuity as a spiritual phenomenon. It is generally accepted that "spirituality" can be distinguished from religion but, for some, religious and non-religious, it is the "S" word and they hate it; for others this is the *sine qua non* of today's progressive politics—the so-called "rise of the religious left" and the emergence of networks of spiritual progressives. (The best known network clusters around the Jewish concept of *tikkun*, meaning repair and restoration of the world; there are equally inspiring Islamic concepts—the one that interests me is the Qur'anic idea of *ta'aruf*, discussed in Chapter Ten, in which the deeper and transformative aspects of conflict are recognised.)

It is hard to define "spiritual", but it involves something "more-than-personal" that lies over or under or beneath or behind the everyday. Often there is a sense of being confronted with something awesome and "bigger" than oneself—more-than-personal. But this is a spirituality that is ubiquitous, hidden in the open, waiting to be discovered, not a result of a "sell" by anyone with ambitions for their religion, sect, or cult.

My anatomy of spirituality (presented much more extensively in the next chapter) suggests that there are different kinds of spiritual deficits or lacks that contemporary Western citizens suffer from. A defect in social spirituality means that the individual has little or no experience of the incredible togetherness that ensues when a group of committed individuals pursue a social or political goal. A defect in craft spirituality means that work is not only without meaning but is also soulless and spiritually damaging. Democratic spirituality is a reworking of the notion of "equality in the eyes of the Lord" and who can doubt that today's polities have resolutely turned their back on paying anything more than lip service to egalitarian goals and ideals.

The focus here is on the fourth element in the anatomy—profane spirituality: sex, drugs, and rock and roll (or popular culture). The thinking here comes from Jung's insight, conveyed to the founders of Alcoholics Anonymous, that alcohol abuse is not only about seeking spirituous drafts but is also a spiritual quest. Herein, I am talking, not only about addictions (and sexual activity can certainly become addictive and compulsive, even statistical) but specifically of the spiritual quest carried by lust and by promiscuity, about "sex as force and not sex as relation" (to use Muriel Dimen's phrase, personal communication, 2007).

This kind of sexual behaviour may be understood in terms of mystical experience. There's something numinous about promiscuous experience, as many readers will know. Overwhelming physical attraction produces feelings of awe and wonderment and trembling. There is a sort of God aroused, a primitive, chthonic, early, elemental God. There is an unfettered experience of the divine.

The idea of a mysticism between people is one by which contemporary theology is captivated. "There is no point at all in blinking at the fact that the raptures of the theistic mystic are closely akin to the transports of sexual union", wrote Richard Zaehner in *Mysticism: Sacred and Profane* (1957). In literature, D. H. Lawrence (1913) fashions a creation myth out of sexual intercourse in *Sons and Lovers*: "His hands were like creatures, living; his limbs, his body, were all life and consciousness, subject to no will of his, but living in themselves."

In Chassidic mysticism, reference is made to a quality known as *hitlahavut*, or ecstasy. Buber held that this quality transforms ordinary knowledge into a knowledge of the meaning of life. For the Chassids, *hitlahavut* expresses itself bodily in dance, where, according to Buber (1957), the whole body becomes subservient to the ecstatic soul. Similarly, William Blake sang that "man has no body distinct from his soul".

In a series of works, Robert Goss (for example, Goss, 2004, p. 59) has been suggesting that behind non-monogamous relating we find the presence of a "promiscuous God", one who loves indiscriminately (if hardly casually). Although Goss is primarily concerned with the reclamation of the bible for LGBT and queer people, his remarkable phrase is a suitable note on which to end this discussion of spirituality and promiscuity.

Promiscuities

Promiscuity is not a monolith—there are often perplexing differences to do with gender, sexual diversity, class, and ethnicity. For reasons of space, I will consider only gender and sexual diversity.

It is sometimes argued that promiscuity as a discourse is written by and for males (this is what Sheila Jeffreys means). But it is interesting to see how much of the non-monogamy literature is written by lesbians. Are we to take this as indicating that it is only where heterosexual relating is concerned that promiscuity is a male game? Surely not. And I had thought that feminism made it clear that most advantages in marriage lay with the husbands who are "obeyed". Yet, at the May '68 conference in 2008, enraged women turned on male members of the audience as much as on the speaker in a moralising frenzy. One said in response to my positing promiscuity as a political as much as a sexual phenomenon: "I cannot believe I've heard you say what I think you've said."

Sexual desire generates an anxiety that calls forth a certitude that is really not at all grounded. I am sure that my thinking about promiscuity suffers from this—and that what might be said against it will suffer from an element of dogmatism as well. I turn my attention to these fascinations of fundamentalism in Chapter Eight. Succinctly, the promise of an end to sexual anxiety is what gives religious fundamentalism its appeal to adherents and its fascination for those who do not see themselves as fundamentalist. We are too quick to theorise why people become fundamentalists without pausing to ask why we are so keen to offer such theorising. Even the critics of fundamentalism are caught up by the seductiveness of its promise of an end to sexual anxiety.

In connection with gender and promiscuity, a particularly interesting document to consider is Catherine Millet's *The Sexual Life of Catherine M.* (2001). One of the most explicit books on sex written by a woman, it recounts Millet's sexual experiences over thirty years. It is an incisive and destabilising work that makes generalising about gender differences in connection with sexuality seem impoverished. Millet tells us that she "exercised complete free will in my chosen sexual life ... a freedom expressed once and for all" (p. 63). She explains how special is the excitement of an encounter with a new lover: "my pleasure was never more intense ... not the first time that I made love with someone, but the first time we kissed; even the first embrace was enough" (p. 84). She is no stranger to jealousy: "I personally have experienced my confrontations with these passionate expressions of jealousy" (p. 74), adding that jealousy is an "injustice".

One passage I found interesting is a reflective memory from Millet's childhood. As a girl, she ran numbers over and over in her mind, and now she is numbering her future husbands: "Could a woman have several husbands at the same time, or only one after the other? In which case, how long did she have to stay married to each one before she could change? What would be an 'acceptable' number of husbands: a few, say five or six, or many more than that, countless husbands?" Questions of time and duration pepper the promiscuity field, no matter the gender of the subject, and I return to time when I come to discuss hypocrisy.

Continuing to look at the plurality of promiscuities, this time with sexual diversity rather than gender in mind, it is interesting to note how often discussions about promiscuity even in quite liberal professional circles of psychotherapists collapse into discussions about promiscuous cottaging on the part of gay men. I have been arguing for many years that therapists have been unconsciously influenced by the media and collective cultural discourses as much as by their own theories concerning the general psychopathology of homosexuality. They have got caught up in a moral panic concerning cottaging and haven't noticed that they've allowed heterosexual promiscuity to fall out of the conversation. Hence, it is well-nigh impossible to manage a reasoned conversation about either promiscuity or cottaging.

Can we make something positive out of this homophobic moral panic? Flip it around? Yes, I think we can if we revisit Leo Bersani's contention in "Is the rectum a grave?" (1987) that the great lesson and gift of gay men to the rest is the massive individualism of promiscuous sex. It is a very specific and powerful form of resistance precisely because there is no political agenda. Bob Dylan made much the same point: "I've never written a political song. Songs can't save the world. I've gone through all that."

Finally, a note on bisexuality and promiscuity. Bisexuals as a group experience specific pressures in relation to promiscuity. I agree with those who insist—for political and psychological reasons—that bisexuality is not a cover for something else and wish to retain the term. They are up against strong opposition. Some will say that bisexuality is but a cover for disavowed homosexuality (if the critic is psychoanalytic), or for politically unacceptable heterosexuality (if the critic is a lesbian or gay activist). As a phenomenon, bisexuality adds a further layer of complexity and paradox to our thinking about monogamy and non-monogamy and the connections between them. As far as psychoanalysis is concerned, Freud's insight of a fundamental bisexuality all too easily gets overlooked (similarly, Jung wrote of a "polyvalent germinal disposition" in the sexual realm).

Promiscuity and imagination

Up to now, we have been discussing historical, political, and spiritual aspects of the promiscuities. But, as a therapist, I know that promiscuity is not only a literal matter. It is also implicated in a whole array of imaginative and metaphorical discourses. For, in addition to the political symbolism, we have to think of promiscuity as symbolising boundary-breaking creativity in both an artistic and a general sense (one could be politically promiscuous, for example).

From a psychological point of view, promiscuity calls up symbolic or metaphorical dimensions of issues of freedom, differentiation from parental and family background, and a new relation to the primal scene (meaning the image we have in our mind of the intimate life or lack of it of our parent(s)). Kleinian psychoanalysis refers to "the couple state of mind", the parents in the mind engaged in fertile and creative intercourse. The intent is to propose a universal symbol of fecundity and mental health generally: "the basis or the fount of personal creativity: sexual, intellectual and aesthetic" (Hinshelwood, 1989, p. 241). But the result is very often a distressingly literal application of the idea. Hence, we must ask: is the couple state of mind, the couple in the mind, always a stable "married" or committed couple? We could also ask: Always a heterosexual couple? Always a couple of the same ethnicity? Not only is this particular Kleinian theory—widely used in British object relations psychoanalysis even beyond the Kleinian group—unquestioningly heteronormative (see Samuels, 2001, pp. 49–51), it is also ferociously conventional.

Revisioned imaginatively, promiscuity holds up the promise—and the threat—of an internal pluralism (Samuels, 1989) always on the brink of collapsing into undifferentiatedness but, somehow, never quite doing so. On a personal level, we are faced with what could be called the promiscuous task of reconciling our many internal voices and images of ourselves with our wish and need to be able to feel, when we desire it so, integrated and to speak with one voice. Returning to bodies for a moment, there is also a metaphorical aspect to promiscuous sex. Promiscuous traces and shadows may be present in constant sexual relationships via the operation of fantasy; and there is a constant element in apparently promiscuous behaviour, if the image of the sexual other remains psychically constant. This takes us back to the Freud-Jung schism over sexuality. Freud spoke for the literal, the instinctual, the causative; Jung for the metaphorical and the teleological, asking "What is sex really for?" Sexual imagery is not only a desire for physical enactment. It is also a symbolic expression of an emotional longing for some kind of personal regeneration through contact with the body of an other.

Support for the idea that there is a promiscuous element in sexual constancy can be found in an unlikely place—Rabbinic Judaism of the early part of the Christian era. In his book *Carnal Israel: Reading Sex in Talmudic Culture*, Daniel Boyarin (1993) explains how the tension between procreative and non-procreative sex operates as a kind of in-house promiscuity. Non-procreative sex is exclusively for pleasure, and pleasure, whether to do with sex or with eating, is regarded by the Rabbis as a good thing. Amongst other revelatory ideas, he shows quite clearly how Judaism strives to heal, as well as force, the split from the body with which it is too easily associated.

In Philip Roth's novel *The Dying Animal* (2001), made into the film *Elegy* in 2008, David Kepesh, academic superstar (and Jew) lives a sexual life of studied promiscuity. But: "No matter how much you know, no matter how much you think, no matter how much you plot and you connive and you plan, you're not superior to sex." Kepesh falls in love with a much younger woman, who will eventually be diagnosed with breast cancer and undergo a mastectomy (he had "worshipped" her breasts). Roth is not making a moral or (pseudo) mature point about the collapse of the promiscuous ideal (nor was the book ever in praise of the promiscuous life). He is underscoring how sexual relating is all about struggle, indeterminacy, and—above all—anxiety. As I said earlier, when considering monogamy, non-monogamy, polyamory and promiscuity, you can't have it all—not even in fantasy! Nevertheless, Roth's *aperçu* in connection with promiscuous sex is worth repeating: "The great biological joke on people is that you are intimate before you know anything about the other person."

Promiscuity and hypocrisy

Hypocrisy is the act of opposing a belief or behaviour while holding the same beliefs or performing the same behaviours at the same time. Hypocrisy is frequently invoked as an accusation in politics and in life in general. Noam Chomsky argued that the key feature of hypocrisy is the refusal to apply to ourselves the same standards we apply to others. So hypocrisy is one of the central evils of our society, promoting injustices such as war and social inequalities in a framework of self-deception.

With these thoughts in mind, I want to turn to my own profession of psychotherapy, both in and of itself and as representative of the wider culture. My accusation is that, when it comes to promiscuity, psychotherapy as an institution and many (but not all) psychotherapists as individuals are hypocritical. In terms of the etymology of the word "hypocrisy", they are play-acting or feigning something. As well as scoring points, I am interested in probing this phenomenon.

It is significant that sex outside of relationship is largely untheorised by analysts and therapists—or, if there is a theoretical position taken, it is invariably in terms of psychopathology, of an alleged fear of intimacy, problems in attachment ("ambivalent attachment") and relationship, perversion, and so on. There is an absence of consideration of what I referred to earlier as sex-as-force (but see Kahr, 2007). Actually, with some notable exceptions, there is very little contemporary psychoanalytic writing on bodily experience at all (but see Orbach, 2009). When Lyndsey Moon (personal communication, 2008) was undertaking research focusing on the needs of bisexual clients, during which she interviewed forty therapists (lesbian, gay male, heterosexual, queer, and bisexual) only three (including the present writer) "actually went anywhere near 'sex' as having a meaning that needs to be talked about or talked through with clients". Moon speculates that the bulk of the therapists were experiencing "much fear of the sexual body and sexual behaviour".

I think it is interesting to ask whether there might be something in the fundamental thinking or set-up of psychotherapy that leads to a carnality-averse conservatism. Certainly, the proliferation of schools in psychotherapy is a gorgeous metaphor for this whole topic: on the one hand, historically, most therapists have been monogamously wedded to one school, yet the field itself is—or so it could be argued—becoming ever more, and ever more threateningly, promiscuous.

We have learned that, for every majority discourse, there is likely to be a subjugated minority discourse. In psychotherapy—as in society—the majority discourse is relational. Hence, the subjugated minority discourse will be the opposite of relational; in the language of this chapter, promiscuous. I have wondered if the silence of psychotherapists on the topic of promiscuity reflects a kind of sexual horror—so they translate everything into a discourse of relationality in which "persons" get split off from "sex".

Putting these ideas—of hypocrisy and a subjugated non-relational discourse—together, exposes the secret moral conservatism of numerous psychotherapeutic clinicians compared to their often very different sexual behaviour as persons. We could begin to understand this more deeply by seeing it as envy on the part of the therapist of the sexual experimentation and out-of-order behaviour related to them by their clients. Many psychotherapists are not overtly judgemental about promiscuous behaviour but tell us that it is a stage or phase of psychosexual development—usually adolescent. As such, the client should grow out of it because it cannot be sustained into middle or old age. It is not hard to see that, aside from whether it is true or part of a general cultural denial about the sexuality of older people, this is far from non-judgemental accepting. It rules out any possibility that promiscuity might function as one template (in classical Jungian terminology, "archetypal structure") for lifelong relational individuation. We don't talk much about the need to hold the tensions between the one and the many when it comes to relationships.

The matter comes to a head when psychotherapists engage with infidelity ("cheating") on the part of their clients. Whilst not denying that some therapists, particularly couple therapists, understand cheating as a systemic phenomenon, the overall psychotherapeutic take on the matter is that it is a symptom of something else, some problem in the cheat, usually of a narcissistic kind. The cheated upon usually feels immense pain and the cheat often feels great guilt. These are strong affects for the therapist to engage with. Hence, unsurprisingly perhaps, what we see in the majority of instances is a counter-resistant valorisation of relational longevity and an utterly literal understanding of "object constancy" at the expense of relational quality. Provided you are in a longstanding relationship, you are, to all intents and purposes, okay. (I take up this point in relation to persons from sexual minorities seeking to train as psychotherapists in Samuels, 2006.)

However, when it comes to sexual desire, time doesn't have all that much to do with it. When I was a schoolboy, we loved Einstein's joke about the theory of relativity: if you kiss a sexy girl for five minutes it feels like five seconds; if you stick your hand in a flame for five seconds it feels like five minutes. In the unconscious, time doesn't work the way it does at the conscious level.

The same is true in relation to sexual desire. One of the most compelling accounts of this is in Ernest Hemingway's *For Whom the Bell Tolls* (1941). Mortally wounded, the Spanish Civil War volunteer, Robert Jordan, is going to cover the escape of his comrades. Lying on the ground, weapon at the ready, he reflects on how he has lived a lifetime of sexual intimacy and a kind of "marriage" with Maria, a girl living with the partisan band, who has been raped by Franco's soldiers. He tries to recall: "Well, we had all our luck in four days. Not four days. It was afternoon when I first got there and it will not be noon today. That makes not quite three days and three nights. Keep it accurate, he said. Quite accurate." And earlier, in passion, "… there is no other now but thou now and now is thy prophet. Now and forever now … there is no now but now." And later, reflectively, "I wish I was going to live a long time instead of going to die today because I have learned much about life in these four days; more I think than in all the other time."

However, erotic time is no truer than any other form of time.

Concluding thoughts

My hope in this chapter was to be able to think afresh in relation to the role of psychotherapy in cultural critique, fashioning that critique this time out of the carnality that we find in promiscuity. Lessons from May '68 and observations from today suggest that, in the West, understandings of the manifold connections, including symbolic connections, between relationality, sexuality, and politics are hindered by negativity and hypocrisy on the part of mental health professionals, academics, critics, and many psychotherapists who seek to impact the political need to pay attention to the limits placed upon their laudable ambition by retrogressive attitudes to promiscuity and sex outside of conventional relational structures of a monogamous nature.

But there was also an additional goal stemming directly from the shift in consciousness I mentioned earlier in the chapter whereby personal change and social change are understood as inseparable. The exploration of the sexual is indeed just that. But as we move on to the social level, and then on to the spiritual level, we are challenged to find out more about suffering, pain, dislocation, alienation and to see how promiscuity might function as a secret spiritual and social passage to the fullest possible healing engagement with a suffering world.

As indicated above, the next chapter deals overtly with spirituality.

CHAPTER SEVEN

Political anatomy of spirituality

Introduction

Spirituality is a big and important theme and it is more political than many people realise. *"Tout commence en mystique et finit en politique* [Everything starts in mysticism and ends in politics], was Charles Péguy's (1910) thought. I have found that, paradoxically, the bigger and more important the theme, the more personal the author's connection to it is likely to be. When I began to have children, as often seems to happen with men, something went on in me which we could call "spiritual". This mixed in with my interests in psychotherapy and politics—so there were now three sides of a coin! After the impact of having children, and the turning towards both organised religion and private religion fatherhood induced in me, I began trying to link up the practice of psychotherapy with my emerging spiritual and existing political concerns.

I will begin the chapter by discussing some general issues and problems of definition. This is necessary when engaging with what I have heard called the "S" word. Next, I will present a second section immodestly entitled "New anatomy of spirituality". The third section is on responsibility, and how that links to psychological and spiritual concerns. The word "responsibility" is important to my thinking. Finally, inevitably, given my Jungian background, I feel that I must talk on the shadow of spirituality. We Jungians started the psychotherapy (and the wider) world off on what seems like its new line of taking spirituality seriously. But we always knew that, alongside the gold, there's something potentially wrong with a spiritual approach. So, paradoxically, Jungians are prominent these days in addressing what's the matter with the spirit, as well as what's great about it.

The "S" word

When Captain Cook's ship *The Endeavour* anchored in Botany Bay a couple of hundred years plus ago, the aboriginal people did not recognise it as a ship. It was simply so big and so different from what they had in their mind as "ship" that they didn't recognise it as such. We don't know what they did think, but we know they didn't think it was a ship. It was only when the smaller longboats—rowing boats—were lowered into the water that the aboriginal observers of this scene realised that there were boats involved, and that there were people in the boats. Spirituality, if we are trying to define it, is something like that. We don't really know that we are in that area until something happens to alert us to it. In Bani Shorter's memorable phrase, everything is susceptible to the sacred (1995). This is a very good one-liner to indicate what happens before you can term something spiritual. Something has to happen that involves you "clocking it", to use the modern argot. For everything can be susceptible to the sacred. It is significant that the lecture upon which this chapter is based was not given in a church or synagogue, ashram, mosque, or temple. We were in a lecture hall in a psychotherapy training organisation. And that setting influenced what we said and what we experienced.

In the new anatomy of spirituality, I seek to advance a vision of spirituality that is regular, ubiquitous, and permeates every aspect of existence. It is not intended to be a lofty, exhortative, sermonising approach. Quite the opposite. My take on spirituality discerns its worm-like nature, not its eagle-like nature. Spirituality as an underneath as well as an over the top thing. And because approaches to spirituality so easily go over the top, it is often better to stay underneath.

So we can scarcely attempt a factual definition of spirituality. We can only give an aspirational one, and therefore whatever we say will be very vague. But there is huge value in vagueness—so much so that there is a philosophical subdiscipline called "vague studies" and even a *Journal of Vague Studies*. We can get terribly hooked on spurious precision when it comes to words, spending much time and energy on the differences between guilt and depression, envy and jealousy, and so on. We speak and write as if we really know, and as if we can really make hard and fast distinctions. It is a kind of love affair of a very perverse kind with precision, and I believe it is deeply problematic, clinically and intellectually. There is something important about staying in the vague for as long as it takes. There are obviously dangers of vagueness but I think that spirituality may not be as dangerous a topic when it is regarded in a vague way as some others because, after all, spirituality has always been something that deconstructs our lives. Long before postmodernism was invented, the spirit was deconstructing daily reality in culture. Hence it is not a problem for me that I am vague about what I mean, or what anyone means by spirituality.

I will leave definition there, caught up in vagueness, thinking of Captain Cook, and the longboats are slowly being lowered into the water, and recognition is gradually dawning.

> Exercise: Imagine yourself as those aboriginal people, watching the long-boats approaching. What are your thoughts and feelings?

A new anatomy of spirituality

There are four aspects to spirituality and the spiritual dimensions of experience that I shall consider: social spirituality, craft spirituality, democratic spirituality, and profane spirituality. In *social spirituality*, people come together to take responsible action in the social sphere, doing this in concert with other people. When this happens, something spiritual comes into being. Being actively engaged in a social, political, cultural, or ethical issue, together with others, initiates the spiritual. As I said earlier, this is a very different perspective from one that would see social spirituality as being something done in the social domain by spiritual people. To the contrary, there is a kind of spiritual rain that can descend on people who get involved in politics and social issues with others—hence "social" spirituality—in a certain kind of way. I call this rain "responsibility".

In analysis and psychotherapy, there are aspects of this social spirituality that we need to consider. Surely therapists no longer indulge in the typical therapeutic manoeuvre, when faced with a client who wants to go on a protest demonstration, of interpreting the anti-parental nature of that move, or understand political participation as defensive, resistant, avoidance, splitting, and so on. If there are people in our profession who still make knee-jerk interpretations of that kind, then what I would say to them is that they are caught up in yesterday's good practice. But the old clinical perspective is today's bad practice and ignores the individuating thrust in the client's political and social commitments and actions. What this means, for example, is that, when you take an initial history or when you meet a client for the first time or when you're interviewing a potential trainee, you don't ask: "Well, why were you so involved in politics when you were eighteen?" Do ask: "Why were you not involved?" And: "Why have you apparently got no social commitments at all? Do you read the news? Do you watch *Newsnight*?" I realise this reverses the way that most therapists have been trained to proceed.

I have written extensively about what happens when political themes enter the psychotherapy dialogue. Succinctly, within certain limits, the engagement of therapist and client in relation to something political can be mutually transformative. This is truly another example of social spirituality. In the therapeutic setting, as the therapist and client engage on 9/11 or the Israel/Palestine situation or the death of Princess Diana, or the decline of the Labour Party, they can find—if they are open to it—a deeply transformative experience that may have a spiritual feel to it, in spite of the fact that the raw material was social, political, controversial, and difficult to deal with for all the technical reasons with regard to suggestion that we know about. For we don't want to foist our politics on our clients. The difficulties involved are highlighted by the fact that there are very few texts that help therapists to work in this area.

Before moving on to discuss craft spirituality, I want to touch on the pressing political problematic of martyrdom in general and suicide bombing in particular. This is a testing topic when thinking about social spirituality. Clearly, for those involved in it, the act of suicide bombing leads to the most profound spiritual transformation on the part of the bomber, no matter how wrong the act is from the point of view of victims of outrages committed by suicide bombers, or of people in the West who simply cannot comprehend how such a thing can come about. Actually, we need to be very careful here, because suicide bombing is not an integral part of any culture that I know of. It is a situational response to a complex sociopolitical situation. But our Western culture cannot comprehend how that came about in other cultures. Martyrdom nudges us up against some of the shadow aspects of spirituality, encouraging us to remember, in any rush to embrace the spiritual and bring it into our work and lives, that martyrdom and acts such as suicide bombing are the most extreme, over-literalised form of social spirituality imaginable. We need to bear this in mind before rushing blindly into political and social action: that there is a place where it can go that is really quite horrific.

Now for *craft spirituality*. My thesis here is a bit startling: holiness is artificial. It is not something that we merely discover or find in our lives, or notice in God or nature, or in the psyche. We make holiness. We make it traditionally by building tabernacles, churches, and by performing rituals—lighting candles, holding each other, and so on. Des Esseintes, as we saw in Chapter Four, would heartily approve of this perspective.

To illustrate this point I want to reflect on the biblical figure of Bezaleel. Many people have never heard of Bezaleel, though there is a Bezaleel Design Institute in Tel Aviv. Bezaleel was the man who actually *made* the Tabernacle and the Ark of the Covenant. He made them to God's precise instructions. When we consider these instructions, we may come to two quite different conclusions. One is that God is the most unbelievable obsessional neurotic! The other is that it really matters to God what is made by us in pursuit of holiness: what materials we use, what dimensions we go for, what bevels, joints, and other technical devices we employ.

> And Bezaleel made the ark of shittim wood, two cubits and a half was the length of it and a cubit and a half the breadth of it, and a cubit and a half the height of it. And he overlaid it with pure gold within and without, and made a crown of gold to it round about. As he cast for it four rings of gold to be set by the four corners of it, even two rings upon the one side of it and two rings upon the other side of it. And he made staves of shittim wood, and overlaid them with gold. And he put the staves into the rings by the side of the ark to bear the ark. (Exodus 37, 1–5)

Such work—maybe, potentially, all work—is a spiritual discipline. In our societies in the West, much work is meaningless and alienating.

Nevertheless, even within the meaninglessness and alienation of contemporary work situations, people often develop and deploy a Bezaleel consciousness. They fashion portable tabernacles and sanctuaries for themselves, usually by ritual, often obsessional seeming: how you line up your pens, what colour pen you prefer to write in, how you close down your computer, which people you greet, and in what way. None of this does away with the appalling barbarism of capitalist work organisation, but all of it shows people trying to enter the domain of craft spirituality. Craft spirituality also spills over into aesthetics. Craft spirituality informs the artistic and creative impulse as well.

A great deal of this is very relevant to modern psychotherapy but, again, there do not seem to be very many books or chapters about it. In fact, there is a lack of psychotherapy literature in connection with work and employment issues. This is somewhat surprising in that clients regularly talk about problems at work. I have hardly ever worked with a client who has unambivalently admired their boss! Rather, those clients that have admired their boss without ambivalence have usually been hopelessly in love with him or her, which isn't much use either.

There are special issues for women in connection with work: the glass ceiling, the appalling continuing differentiation of wage rates, the enormous difficulty in getting successive Chancellors of the Exchequer and the Inland Revenue to engage with the issue of tax relief for child care, which, although it should not be a "woman's issue", impacts more on the social and work lives of women than of men. A psychotherapist who does not engage with a woman client in those areas is not only guilty of a social omission, he or she is guilty of a spiritual omission as well, because work—craft spirituality—cannot be split off from spirituality as such.

There certainly are craft spirituality issues for men as well. Most private practice psychotherapists don't see many manual labourers. But we do see the children of manual labourers. That's the harsh social fact about it, in private practice anyway. Have you noticed how difficult it can be for the more successful son to come to terms with what that means in relation to the apparently less successful father, who may be by now part of a long-term unemployed rust-belt declining industry in the North?

For both men and women, there is a very overt spiritual theme that has to do with work, which has been given the unprepossessing tag of work-life balance. (I must declare an interest here as a former Trustee of the Work-Life Balance Trust.) There is a sense in which work-life balance may be the issue of our time. This includes more than having an annual go-home-on-time day! It's much more than just addressing the chronic workaholism of the population—something that most psycho-therapists know about as well, because it's a problem a lot of us have. Getting your work and your personal life into some kind of balance is a spiritual matter and not only a social matter. Without decent work-life balance, can anyone really flower as a spiritual being, as a person with a soul? Yet work-life balance is not really discussed by psychothera-pists. It is discussed by occupational psychologists, of course, and it's increasingly interesting to economists and accountants, for companies that have effective policies on work-life balance do very well financially. Profit is by no means the right reason to go in for work-life balance but there is a bottom-line aspect that makes it more likely that this move-ment could have some social and political success. My main point here, when discussing craft spirituality, is to suggest that work-life balance be understood more and more as a spiritual and psychological matter.

I hope it is becoming clearer what I am aiming at in the chapter. This is a contemporary take on spirituality, so that it can become "useful", if you like, in apparently non-spiritual places: in the therapy room, in society, and in people's work lives.

Third in the anatomy is *democratic spirituality*. This involves bringing back on to all kinds of agendas—personal, political, and clinical—the idea of absolute equality. In all the discussions about equality of out-come and equality of opportunity, something has got lost. And that is this notion of absolute equality, which used to be called traditionally "equal in the eyes of the lord". We are all equal in the eyes of the lord. This is a powerful idea, because it underpins any protest about eco-nomic inequality and the situation in the wider world in which women and children die because of economic policies undertaken by their gov-ernments at the behest of the World Bank or the International Monetary Fund. Democratic spirituality puts the notion of absolute equality, in all its glorious impracticability, back on to the agenda. In particular, demo-cratic spirituality is an attempt from the spiritual end of the spectrum to engage with poverty, economic injustice, and economic inequality. From the standpoint of psychotherapy, there's a great deal that should be said but usually is not. With some notable exceptions in humanistic and integrative psychotherapy, and of people working in transcultural psychotherapy, psychotherapists in Britain, especially psychoanalytical therapists and psychoanalysts, are not adept at working with power issues in therapy. We still tend to prefer to put the client's challenge to us down to their trouble with a powerful mother, omnipotent breast, phallic mother, great mother, terrible mother, or a castrating, law-giving father who says "no". But there are power issues in the therapy relationship itself which, if overlooked, prevent a certain kind of spiritual or transpersonal communication between therapist and client from taking place. The idea of absolute equality, though impractical, I admit, is an ethical penetration of the psychotherapy relationship which leads to an enhancement of the spiritual experience that it can generate.

A couple of final points in relation to democratic spirituality. The first reflects the influence of psychoanalytic thinking on spiritual thinking. In relational psychoanalysis, which is the promising recent variant of psychoanalysis that is coming into this country from the United States associated with the name of Stephen Mitchell, the tools exist to describe a particular kind of democratic psychological relationship with God. If you like, this is a relational spirituality, in which one might surrender to the divine, but without masochistically submitting to it. Surrender, but not submission. This relational spirituality, coupled with what I have been saying about democracy and spirituality, is very suggestive and important for therapists. We discern a non-submissive, non-masochistic sense of veneration, in ourselves and our clients, to use the evocative language of Rosemary Gordon's very important work on this topic (1987). Being able to worship without having to masochistically submit to authority is a part of contemporary spirituality.

The last in the four is *profane spirituality*. Profane spirituality is about drugs, sex, and rock and roll. Jung replied to a query by Bill W., the founder of Alcoholics Anonymous, with a critically important letter (1961) in which he advanced the idea that alcoholism was a spiritual quest that had gone off the rails. This insight can be applied to so many other addictions, up to and including shopping and workaholism. For the avoidance of doubt, perhaps I should make it plain that I am not saying that shopping is a spiritual activity. What I am saying is that there is a strand of energy in the act of shopping that connects to all the searching and questing that spirituality is commonly associated with.

Regarding rock and roll, I mean to propose in a shorthand way that we can locate the spiritual drive in popular culture, not only music but also movies, and sport as well. There is a spiritual component here, not really different from that which the intellectual authorities of the world locate in Rembrandt or Wagner or art from the Orient. There is something in what the kids do, and what we did when we were kids (and, I hope, we still do) that should not be put down by reference to "the canon", as they call it in the big debate about what you should study in literary studies. The canon is Shakespeare and Dickens. The anti-canon is Danielle Steele. Though you can get MAs in America in Danielle Steele, I am not going down that track. What I want to say is that, if one talks about profane spirituality, popular culture plays a central part.

Profane spirituality involves sex and sexuality, as we saw in the previous chapter on promiscuity. There is usually a spiritual level in deeply intimate relationships. Psychotherapists need to say more about what it does to the human spirit to enter the domains of alterity, to really confront the other in her or his ethical otherness. And how this leads to self-discovery, and how God-discovery weaves its way through all of it. But I am not only referring to relationships, I am thinking about sex itself—orgasmic, orgiastic, rapturous, to the point of mysticism. That is important because so many mystics write about their mystical experiences in the most frank sexual imagery. There is something about the sex act—just sex as a drive, not sex as part of a relationship—that people who engage with the spiritual would often like to overlook. Here one must (still, regrettably, have to) assert that homosexual sex acts bring a spiritual element with them just as often, or just as seldom, as heterosexual sex acts. Profane spirituality is decidedly not something that goes on only within the sanctity of heterosexual marriage.

The implications of profane spirituality for psychotherapy are enormous. Psychotherapists are becoming fascinated with the body, with neuro-biology, neuro-anatomy, and cognitive neuroscience. Some even refer to neuro-psychoanalysis. It is argued that the structure of the brain can be affected by what happens to an individual as a client in therapy. It is also argued that something happens to the structure of the brain in the early months and years of life. Our psychology has become absolutely obsessed with the body. And yet body therapy hardly gets a look in. There is something very problematic here. We need to go back to those old debates about touch and movement in therapy. The body is the grounding for spirit. But just because it is such a grounding should not mean that we then put it on one side as something noticed but not taken up. We know about the body and countertransference, and how the somatic states in the therapist are really useful in understanding the psychological states in the client. We know about psychosomatic medicine. In fact, we often say indecent things in our clinical chapters that offend the sufferers of various illnesses by proclaiming them to be little more than depression in disguise.

So we are correctly body obsessed. Yet how many of us have regularly—not just occasionally—noticed the breathing of our clients? How many therapists reading this have observed the breathing of the client in therapy? How many therapists have actually said anything about it? Some have, of course. Or explored your own? Again, some have. Some time ago, I decided to systematically observe the breathing of my clients and my own and I noted that, if I do this, the therapy dialogue alters whether I do anything with what I've noticed or not. Sometimes, I do speak about it. It seems to me absurd to have all these developments that take the whole field in a bodily direction, except in relation to practice! William Blake said: "Man has no body distinct from his soul." So can there really be any psychotherapy worth its salt that isn't in some sense a body psychotherapy?

I want to end this section on sex and sexuality with a few transcultural points in connection with the body—because one of the interesting things about the body is that there is no such thing as a body. There is only my body or your body in this particular society in this particular year. We should listen to colleagues who do transcultural or intercultural work. Here in the West, we talk about people somaticising their depression: they are depressed and they produce a whole variety of physical symptoms that are really their depression in disguise. At a famous conference of psychoanalysts in India in the late fifties, one of the Indian participants got up and said: "Actually the trouble is not that people somaticise depression, but that you in the West psychologise it." For us (he said), depression is always already a bodily state. The Western approach to depression, before and after Freud's "Mourning and Melancholia" (1917), is the odd thing in the situation here. Once, in Brazil, I met with indigenous people, and one person said to me, as he had probably said to other tourists (yet it is still worth repeating): "We always had spirit, it was you Westerners, the Portuguese, who brought the body." And everybody knows about how mind, spirit, and body have got separated in Western culture. There is much to learn from non-Western sources about this kind of thing (see Samuels, 2002).

Responsibility

The words responsible or responsibility come from the Latin root *spondere*—to pledge. As noted, the dictionary refers to being held to account, being morally responsible for one's actions and, interestingly, answerable to a criminal charge. If you are responsible for something, then there's a perpetual sense that you are answering a charge, that something is "wrong". These etymological roots mean that responsibility can only ever be a dialectical business. One cannot really be responsible if there isn't another with whom or towards whom one is responsible.

People give themselves much too hard a task when it comes to responsibility. They lose sight of the very important psychological, spiritual, and political notion of good-enoughness. My preference is not to use Winnicott's notion of good-enoughness developmentally. To me, there is a whole possibility of refreshing the spiritual and political vocabulary bound up with the notion of good-enoughness, for example, that good-enough leader, who admits that she or he will fail and sees as their primary task the management of failure, who will try—to play with Winnicott's words—to fail the country in the country's own way. Or the good-enough citizen, who recognises that alone one can do so little but with other people one can achieve much more. I suggest "responsible-enough" should be good-enough for most of us. This idea brings with it a change that makes notions of responsibility more viable, more achievable. Good-enoughness in relation to one's sense of responsibility involves self-forgiveness and atonement. And these things are what lie behind the Hebrew word *tikkun*, meaning the restoration and repair of the world. But we cannot rehabilitate the world if we are so hard on ourselves that we see ourselves only as permanently fractured. We can only move to restore and repair the world on the basis of self-forgiveness and atonement. Back to Beckett: "No matter. Try again. Fail again. Fail better." We have to try to fail better, recalling Rumi's words: "Failure is the key to the kingdom".

The shadow of spirituality

There is something about spirituality that is not all right. It is not just that there's a good "mature spirituality", to use the unfortunate title of a recent book, for that would imply there was an immature spirituality. I think there's *something* not right about spirituality per se, locked in there with all the beauty and holiness. Look at the evidence. Spiritualty is deployed by collective, mass movements of particularly nasty kinds. It is there in every fascistic movement as well as in less dramatic mass movements. One can see why, because the spirit is part of the collective. But, because it's part of the collective, spirit is easily assimilable to mindless and destructive political and social actions. I wouldn't say this is due to humanity's defects, that the spirit is all right but we poor inadequates misuse it. It is more fundamental, this shadow of spirit, and there is something in spirit that is permanently not grounded and hence can cause damage. When spirit is not grounded (and, on this thesis, it never is wholly grounded), it gets you into states where you will do things that are horrible before you can catch yourself and stop yourself from doing it.

"Spiritual people" often display indifference to suffering. I believe this is also true in the psychotherapy world, where you have people who are very compassionate to their clients, but extremely uncompassionate to any individuals beyond that, including colleagues. Because a person's mind is on higher or deeper things, you are not going to be terribly concerned with other people. Then we need to recall the way in which spiritual leaders seem so often to go on power trips. This is the problem of the guru, about which there's a considerable literature now, and the root literature for many studies of the psychological kind of guru-ism are those researches of violent gangs that were done in the fifties. Everything that was discovered about violent gangs and their leaders in New York City in the 1950s is directly relevant to the study of guru-led cults that have gone completely off the rails in the past fifty years.

Another element in the shadow of spirituality is elitism. The spiritual one feels better than other people. That's part of the appeal of fundamentalism. Why make vows of obedience and humility and poverty if not to control their opposites? All taboos imply the impulses that need to be taboo-ed. Spiritual people who take vows of humility are acknowledging in the act of taking the vow of humility that, if allowed to get away with it, they will be anything but humble. Such is the elitism that is the ineluctable shadow of spirituality.

To illustrate spiritual elitism, I will mention something from my own experience. After my father died, chapters arrived including a buff file that had on the outside the legend "Andrew Samuels—writings". In this file were letters and so forth dating from long before I became a writer.

In this file was a letter that I wrote when I was on what we now call a gap year in Swaziland, Southern Africa. I went out there, lied about my age, and got a job in the colonial civil service as an assistant district commissioner. I went off into the bush to do what we called a "human resources survey" in connection with rural community development. There, I wrote a letter to my parents slagging off the Western family in general, and ours in particular, saying how I had discovered, living in the ad hoc extended family that one finds when you go into an African village, and they are very pleased to see you and take you into their homes, that here, in Africa, are families where people do get on! I wrote about the impact this was having on me. And I used the word spirituality in that connection. I remember being terribly terribly pleased with this letter. It is long, elaborate, and adeptly (if destructively) put together. But when I read it again in my father's file, I thought: You little shit! What nasty, elitist side-swipes. What grandiosity. What an abuse of the spiritual dimension of life.

Continuing to explore the personal aspect of the shadow of spirituality, I would like to share a dream of mine, which, as I understand it, is about the body and about my struggle to keep spirit and body in some kind of related linkage. It is my initial dream from my analysis, dating from September 1971. I dreamt this on the exact date the Germans invaded Poland in 1939—and my family comes originally from Poland.

> I am on the deck of a Soviet-style (but not Russian) ice-breaker. We are in a northern sea, the ice-covered Baltic, or the Skagerrak, or somewhere up there. The sea is flat, ice, and the ice-breaker is breaking the ice. I am on the bridge of it. I look out and I see shooting up through the ice great gushing spouts of volcanic-type flame, but there's no volcano, mostly golden-coloured flame. I am awestruck by the concatenation, the combination of the natural landscape, of the flat ice, and the unreal (from the literal point of view) thrusting upwards of the golden spouts of flame. Something makes me look down at my body. I am naked. I look at my genitals and there I see a rather crude leather pouch covering them and compressing them. I reach down and, very gently remove it, and put it on one side.

I return to this dream over and over again, not only in connection with these writings on spirituality, but in connection with many aspects of my life. I share it because the note on which I want to end the chapter is about the central significance and challenge of facilitating the body side of things and the spirit side of things into a dialogical relationship.

In the next chapter, the area of concern is still, broadly speaking, connected to spirituality (and to religion), but in a rather more sceptical and jaundiced vein.

CHAPTER EIGHT

The fascinations of fundamentalism

This short chapter continues to explore the interconnections between politics and spirituality. The chapter is not about why people become fascinated by fundamentalist movements and join up to them. It is in fact about "our" fascination with the figure of the fundamentalist, usually Islamic, and overlooking Jewish, Christian, and Hindu fundamentalists. I also want to fray the neat and tidy divide between "fundamentalists" and "us".

In a nutshell, I propose that the fascination to (apparent) non-fundamentalists is that some profound human psychological themes and tendencies are activated. There is, therefore, generic human ground between the fundamentalists and us. But, as we will see, there clearly are many more fundamentalisms than the usual kind, buried in apparently more tolerant milieux.

I say that the fascination of fundamentalism to others, primarily in so-called liberal and allegedly more tolerant cultures, is that fundamentalists are like us—only more so! Fundamentalism and fundamentalists represent an out-of-reach, idealised, literalised, and concretised version of ourselves—what psychoanalysis might recognise as a contemporary mirroring other of an especially problematic kind.

The four themes that I see as underpinning the appeal and the fascination of fundamentalism are: sexuality, sacrifice, morality, and aggression.

Behind the gender certitudes of fundamentalism lie the usual immense anxieties over sexuality. Fundamentalism settles these anxieties with its literalising clarity. In fact, it is a main feature of fundamentalism that it tips the balance between literalism and symbol in favour of the former in all its solidly reassuring concreteness. This literalism constitutes the psychological fingerprint of fundamentalism—and it is literally literal, given the prominent position of the Book in many religious and political fundamentalisms.

As far as sexuality is concerned, this anxiety-settling clarity is what enables it to structure the relations between women and men in a way that is usually, though not always, unchallenged. Behind physical sex is a search for meaning and context, which fundamentalism provides. When sex goes off in a relationship, it is often because of a catastrophic loss of its meaning. I could invent a new diagnostic category here: "meaning deficit disorder", which fundamentalism offers to cure.

To summarise this section on sexuality: fundamentalism appeals to the fundamentalists and fascinates us in its particularly reassuring engagement with the overwhelming and upsetting anxieties provoked by sex.

Sacrifice of oneself for another or something other—such as a cause, community, nation, or religion—is a widespread psychological, historical, and anthropological theme, both literally and symbolically. We say "no pain, no gain". Sacrifice leads to renewal (for example, of the earth or soil), to love and relatedness, and to the survival and flowering of the community. Sacrifice lies at the heart of Abrahamic religious symbolism (thinking of Abraham and Isaac and the ram). It is, of course, a far older religious phenomenon than that. And sacrifice is a central element in fundamentalist discourse.

Let's take a brief further look at the depth psychology of sacrifice (this was introduced in Chapter Three in connection with sustainable economics). In Jungian theory, ego-consciousness is understood as eventually being too atomistic, rationalistic, and arrogantly wedded to logic for the subject's individuation. The ego has to be, as it were, "sacrificed" for movement in the self to take place. In my own work, I've extraverted this Jungian insight to suggest that much the same could go on in the social realm. For example, citizens have to sacrifice the dubious regressive pleasures of passive and infantile dependence on heroic male leaders so as to realise their own potential for collaborative politics under sibling leadership. (When I spoke about how this thought about sacrifice in politics was relevant for women on BBC Radio's *Woman's Hour*, the programme producers got a substantial appreciative response.)

To summarise this section on sacrifice: fundamentalism appeals to the fundamentalists because of the expectation of benefits and gains for the community. It fascinates us because of the connection to change and improvement on both personal and social levels.

Turning now to morality: psychoanalysis, ethology, cognitive science, and genetics are moving into an uneasy agreement that humans are not born amoral (to use British psychoanalyst Donald Winnicott's idea). There seems to be something like a skeletal, ineluctable moral sensibility in humans, made flesh by human and social relationality. Obviously, the details and particulars of moral and ethical codes and behaviours vary very widely, historically and geographically.

The idea I am floating is that, in its outspoken espousal of codified public and private moralities, fundamentalism does not in fact have an uphill struggle to be heard. There is a marked resonance always already.

Of course, it is often a very harsh and rigid morality that fundamentalisms of the religious variety promote—what I call "original morality". This original morality is devoid of the possibility of debate and discussion, of forgiveness of self and other, of atonement and reparation. There are no exceptions to the rule. Self-congratulatory elitism is the outcome even when the discourse is one of humility and the avoidance of pride. The whole world-view is highly literal, with no room for symbol or metaphor—which is why actual punishment lies at the core of this kind of morality.

What is missing is the other side of moral process—what I call "moral imagination"—in which forgiveness, atonement, and reparation are positively valued. For moral imagination to flourish, exceptions are the rule!

Yet, were moral process only to consist of moral imagination, it would be too slippery and unreliable. So, just as moral process based only on the cruel, codified pomposities of original morality is insulting to human creativity, moral process based only on imagination is going to be far too tricksy.

For there to be a full moral process, there needs to be a dialectical interplay between the fundamental, ineluctable, rigid original morality and the more generous, tolerant moral imagination. This is not an easy balance to strike, as we all know from daily life. I hope it is clear what I am getting at here—the mix between what you might call standards or rules and something that responds to the urgencies of a difficult situation.

To summarise this section on morality: fundamentalism appeals to the fundamentalists because it confers a sense of moral superiority. It fascinates us because it poses a question that is central in lived experience: How to get a balance between the certitude of original morality and the flexibility of moral imagination? (I turn to this question in the final chapter of the book.)

Most liberally minded people discuss fundamentalism in terms of its aggression, which is very convenient for them, a projection of the shadow of the intellectual! They see fundamentalism as aggressive towards other ways of knowing and being, or of worshipping and relating. This seems a bit obvious and self-congratulatory, as if Western societies were nothing but open-minded and welcoming of the stranger. I am not sure that a vision of fundamentalism as aggressive to the outside is the whole picture, and I want to review the same ground from a rather different angle.

I want to suggest that in its avoidance of difference and diversity, in its turning its back on tolerance, fundamentalism is actually *terrified* of aggression. In fact, I further suggest that fundamentalism seeks to manage aggression out of existence.

Let me develop this a bit more. Tolerance of and a vital relation to difference involve inevitable degrees of conflict and aggression. Tolerance will imply aggression because there are always going to be misunderstandings, disappointments, struggles for power and resources. Now, if there is no philosophy of tolerance and no vital relation to difference, there will, on a very important level, be no consequent conflict and aggression. On this reading, fundamentalism can be understood is an anti-aggressive discourse—though certainly not one that we should praise simply for that reason given that it is fear of ordinary, healthy-enough aggression that is the problem for fundamentalism.

It's worse, actually. We should not praise fundamentalism for seeking to manage aggression because, if you can't face aggression, then you have to steer clear of anything to do with tolerance, difference, and diversity. Okay, so fundamentalism helps a person to avoid the aggression of encountering something different. But isn't that a terrible loss for that person. Aren't they then deprived of the benefits of difference and diversity? A superficially easier but less rich life is guaranteed when the problems of tolerance are bypassed or frozen. If you search out the etymological roots of the word "tolerance" in Latin, it comes from the verb meaning "to bear," and that in turn comes from the Greek verb meaning "to suffer". Tolerance is hard and painful work. Intolerance is a helluva lot easier.

I realise that to accept the claim that fundamentalism has a problem with aggression—the exact opposite of the problem it is usually thought to have—won't be easy. So I want to explain this thinking yet a little more.

The basic idea comes from Islam. I have been on a steep learning curve here, due to the interfaith and inter-religion work that I am currently doing. As a Jewish man, I have found an engagement with Islam a highly emotional experience. In print, I have suggested—to my cost—that Islam has the potential to be more than the shadow of the West; that it may have something to teach us about a one-sided mode of life (materialism, tawdry sex including trafficking, lack of spiritual values and integrity in politics). Such thinking may help to deepen and nuance the debate over "the rise of the religious left" that many people are talking about in the States and, in slightly different language, in Britain.

Let me quote once again 49:13 of the Koran, where we find the *ta'aruf* verse that I referred to in Chapter Two. To remind readers, *ta'aruf* means "that you might come to know one another": "Oh Mankind, we have created of you male and female, and have made you peoples and tribes, that you might come to know one another."

In terms of a discussion on intolerance and tolerance, this is a fresh take on difference, on relationality, on the value to the subject of otherness, and on the religious and psychological importance of multilateralism and inter-culturalism.

We know that men and women, and peoples and tribes, enter into conflict as they fail to resolve their differences. We see an acceptance and valorisation of misunderstanding and conflict in the service of encountering difference and diversity and getting to know one another. As I said, *ta'aruf* seems to me to be rather different from Judaism's Tower of Babel or Christianity's universal salvation via acceptance of Christ.

To summarise this section on aggression: fundamentalism offers fundamentalists a chance to avoid the knock-on effects of an encounter with difference, which are an experience of conflict and aggression within the self. Aggressive rhetoric and pronouncements are not the same as the ordinary reciprocal aggression engendered by a meeting with something strange and new. For those of us who do not see ourselves as fundamentalists, our fears, hopes, and aspirations about benefiting from an encounter with difference are played out on the pitch we call fundamentalism.

In this short chapter, I have tried to show how the reasons why fundamentalism appeals to fundamentalists are the reasons why fundamentalism fascinates us. I have suggested that these groups called "fundamentalists" and "us" have quite a lot in common from a depth psychology point of view. I demonstrated this with reference to sexuality, sacrifice, morality, and aggression.

The next two chapters move away from the politics of spirituality and religion to take a look at the politics of parents and children.

CHAPTER NINE

The plural father*

Introduction

Conferences on fathers and fathering are quite often highly politicised affairs. Gender wars are waged. Moral panic is in the air. People's personal histories get into the process. Tradition is assailed by innovation and vice versa. All go a little crazy due to media interest and there are sometimes demonstrations and counter-demonstrations taking place outside the meeting hall, and a good deal of stress and anxiety inside the hall. When the father—or men—is the theme, there really is a coming together of the political and the personal. At such moments, we can see clearly something that is usually hidden: developmental psychology and mental health perspectives on family process implicated in political dispute over "the family" (see Samuels, 1993, 2001). That may be why Jesse Jackson threatened (on an open mic) to squeeze Barack

---

*Publication note: This chapter is an updated and revised version, in which I answer my critics, of "The good enough father of whatever sex", which was part of my 2001 book *Politics on the Couch: Citizenship and the Internal Life*.

Obama's nuts in 2008 when the then candidate seemed to pillory African-American fathers and families.

In this chapter, I discuss the psychological and sociopolitical implications of changes in the pattern in which only women look after small babies. The outcome will depend to a great extent on the successful fostering of a cultural climate in which parenthood and work may co-exist. A key sociopolitical aspect of this concerns the possibility of working towards more co-operative and less hierarchical forms of political and social organisation. I argue that such developments could become more achievable were clearer understandings of male sexuality in general and paternal sexuality in particular to evolve. How we define and what we expect from good-enough families, needs to be enhanced and expanded to include lone parent families and other "transgressive" modes of family life such as lesbians and/or gay men parenting together.

The father in contemporary Western political debate

I propose to break up the monolith called "father" by introducing two rather unusual versions of the father on whom I have been working for over thirty years. I call these figures the "good-enough father" and the "father of whatever sex". Back in the eighties, the good-enough mother was the key parent for psychoanalysis and for developmental psychology. So to steal Donald Winnicott's tag "good-enough" for the father upset the applecart then and, sometimes, still does today.

The suggestion that fathers are not necessarily male has always been loaded. Why do I continue to use the word "father" in relation to a woman? The idea is to show that there is both more and less to fathers than moral panics about lone parenthood suggest. Scanning the huge and passionate debate about lone parenthood in most Western countries with a psychologically attuned eye, the following thought comes to mind. We are witnessing a damaging and misleading idealisation of fathers and the roles men play in families. It is folly to base policy on this idealisation. But the fact that there is such an official idealisation gives current political debate about lone parenthood a very psychological character. The politics are psychological and the psychology has become highly political. It is on this psycho-political level that my tactic of referring to "the good-enough father of whatever sex" is located.

What drives the continuing stigmatisation of women who parent alone in many Western countries is a failure to come to terms with the incipient collapse of some (not all!) of the pillars that used to support male domination of society—a collective failure that has, as we know, left many men utterly unsure of their personal roles. Men still have the power, of course, but they lack fixed identity. This unsettles them so much that they find living with it difficult or impossible, as one understanding of the British suicide figures shows: male suicide has almost doubled; female suicide has declined. It cannot simply have been austerity and unemployment, for we have had recessions before.

It seems that all that the government, some academics, sections of the media, and many analysts and therapists are able to do is to yearn for the return of the father as a source of stability, discipline, and order in the family and, by some kind of alchemy, in society as well. This yearning persists in spite of the fact that the so-called "traditional" family was a very short-lived phenomenon (if it existed at all). The family has always mutated in a duet with economic and industrial organisation (see Seccombe, 1993). That is why it is so important not to fall for the temptations of underclass theory (Murray, 1990) and pillory today's lone parents and their families—never mind the scarcely hidden racism in that tendency. It is supine, ridiculous, and nasty to yearn for yesterday's ideal family. That family, source of so much misery, was but one staging post on a long journey. Too much nostalgia makes you go blind; you can't see the truth for the tears.

In this yearning, the father is presented as concerned primarily with the right kind of character formation. A first leader in the London *Times* newspaper back in 1993 showed this up very well by bemoaning the absence of fathers as a "moral presence" in the family, and such thinking is still prevalent. It could have been written today in several Western countries. The trouble is that, when faced with thinking like this, there is, in progressive circles, a vacuum where new ideas should exist.

My view is that, if we worked out the detail of these fresh approaches, we would not end up with a set of views and values that would leave lone parent, fatherless families in the lurch. These new ideas about fatherhood stress the father's active, direct emotional involvement with his children from the earliest age. The new models of fatherhood support an egalitarian, co-operative, non-hierarchical family rather than just seeking a pointless restoration of father and his authority as the (flawed) source of rules and regulations—not to mention the father as the source of sexual and physical abuse of women and children.

As a clinician who has carried out research into lone parent families for four decades, I observe that many of the most disturbed people I see in analysis come from highly conventional backgrounds with two long-married parents who may even both still be alive. Hence, I simply cannot agree that there are any *inevitable* damaging psychological outcomes from living in a lone parent family. This point would be even stronger were lone parent families to be given adequate resources, approval, and support from the community. When we talk about resources, we should perhaps think of more than money, housing, and so forth—though these are clearly the main things. We could also think, for example, of what it does to the evolving personality of a child to know that the set-up at home is being attacked out there in the real, adult world as inferior, bad, mad, and needing control. My own children certainly picked up quite specific social and political values and assumptions like these from TV before they were three years old (and see Miedzian, 1992, pp. 207–236 for a survey of the influence of television on social attitudes).

Playing the father role

Returning to the father, as I see it there are two crucial psychocultural implications of these new approaches to fathering. The first has to do with the passionate debate that rages over the consequences (or lack of them) of lone parenthood for child development, especially or even exclusively when the lone parent is a woman. We could call this, for convenience, the lone mother question. The second implication has to do with the equally passionate debate over what fathering is these days, even when it is done by men. We could call this the crisis in fatherhood question.

The insight I want to develop, and around which much of this piece revolves, is that responding to these two apparently different questions—the lone mother question and the crisis in fatherhood question—leads us in a surprisingly similar direction. Addressing one question helps us in engaging with the other. Both questions stimulate responses based on the same search, which is to find out what fathers do do, or can do, that is life-affirming and related, beyond being a "moral presence".

If we do this, then I think we can begin to create and assemble a sort of psychological information pool or resource for women bringing up children on their own or women bringing up children together with other women. Such women are truly fathers of whatever sex when the father is revisioned as being able to be less like a patriarch. Immediately, we undermine everything that most modern Western societies assign or wish to assign to men. Anatomy would cease to determine parental destiny and the lone mother question is completely reframed.

There is a crucial sequence in which this project has to be carried out. Initially, we have to find out more about fathers, then move on to see if we can depict the father in a less hypermasculine way, and then finally address women. To women: Can you do these things that male fathers do? Do you *want* to do them? The invitation is for women to assert their capacities to be fathers of whatever sex, which would surely make them good-enough fathers, rather than setting them up to fail as phony ideal fathers. We should not forget that men fail to be ideal fathers, too.

I am not anticipating that women would choose to perform all of any list of fatherly functions, nor would they necessarily perform these functions in *precisely* the same way that men might perform them. But would that matter? Some would say that might be a pretty good thing! Difference does not always mean deficit.

Gathering enough information about the father might enable women to decide how much of it they could do by and for themselves. This is why I give a twist to the usual formulation and propose that we start to call women who parent alone good-enough fathers. I am sure that many women who parent alone or parent together with other women are doing a lot of being a good-enough father of whatever sex without naming it as such. This group of women represents an incalculably valuable resource. We need to set up national educational campaigns fuelled by some of these thoughts about gender politics and organised in some way around the twin images of the good-enough father and the father of whatever sex. This could herald a whole new approach to parenting that plugs into the fluidity in gender roles that has evolved since the Second World War and which is not going to be wished and/ or legislated away by governments. You can't pass acts of parliament that control what people feel and experience. That is what the collapsed totalitarian regimes in the East learned the hard way.

To those who have a negative gut reaction to the idea that women can be good-enough fathers and play the father's role, I say: Men, too, only *play* the father's role. Fathering does not come naturally to men, along with penises and stubble—it has to be learned, and every new father finds there are rules in our society about how to do it; there is a masquerade of manliness, a male masquerade, to adapt Joan Rivière's term (Rivière, 1929). Women who father as good-enough fathers of whatever sex may teach a thing or two to men who father—who knows? I remember my daughter setting up a game with me by saying "You be the daddy, Daddy"—and then, at some point in our family play, announcing "Now I'll be the daddy, Daddy".

This is the bottom line lived-experience point arising from all the academic work on the cultural construction of gender and its roles (e.g., Foucault, 1976; Weeks, 1985). Men already play the role of fathers as much as women will come to play the role of fathers. And they play it differently at different times and in different places; parenting has pronounced multicultural aspects. It is surely significant how much we all use the word "role" in relation to parenting. So, for the sake of completeness, I want to reverse what I have been saying. Women who look after very small children are *playing* at being mothers, playing the role of mother. Motherhood, too, is not as natural as some people continue delusively to think it is. Maternity and paternity have evolving histories.

What of the second question, the question of the crisis in fatherhood, what fatherhood is and means for men? What happens if we make use of the same words and images but this time with a focus on fatherhood and men? We certainly need to make the role of the male parent more interesting and meaningful for those younger men who have started to reject a dictatorial, "Jurassic" style of fathering. Refusal of male dominance by women, coupled with some men's beginning search for inspiring ideas about manhood and fatherhood, are crucial social and psychological changes on which the debate about fathers should be focusing. There is scarcely a social critic (feminist or non-feminist) who has not explored the question of what would happen if fathers were to become more active parents of very small children.

Men are being scrutinised nowadays in ways that hitherto they have scrutinised everyone and everything else. "Men" has become a category, one of many, and not some sort of privileged vantage point. This huge change in Western consciousness concerning men does not mean that men and women now have identical agendas; I have become suspicious of simplistic calls for partnership between the sexes. Men will not give up their power that easily. But the notion of partnership between the sexes in pursuit of social justice remains as an ideal at which to aim.

Lone parent families need more resources, support, and approval from the community (and not less, as some politicians in Britain are currently proposing in an attempt to use the tax and welfare systems in a form of social engineering to deal with the problem lone parent families are perceived to present). In addition, we need to work out strategies for making sure that lone parents and their children are not simply seen as victims. Writing as a man, a father, an analyst, and long-time researcher of lone parenthood and fathering, I have come to see that it is not the actual maleness of the person from whom we obtain fathering that is the key issue. This does not mean denying difference between the sexes when it comes to parenting. The main thing is that what happens in the relationship between the father of whatever sex and her or his children be good enough.

I will try to sketch out some ideas about what fathers do, or can do, that go beyond discipline, order, morality, and so forth. The aim is to work on two levels: as a resource for women who parent alone; and as an agenda for contemporary men who want to father in a new way that is psychologically realistic. To underscore this point, consider a series of (trick) questions. When a man takes care of a very small baby, what should we call what he does? Is it *fathering*, part of an enhanced and expanded definition of father? Or is it *mothering*, because looking after the newborn is what mothers traditionally do? Or is it a bit of both? Similarly, if a woman lays down the law in a family, is she *mothering*, part of an enhanced and expanded definition of a mother? Or is she *fathering*, because laying down the law is what fathers traditionally do? Or is it a bit of both? It can seem very frightening how totally our language for parenting has collapsed; that is why some want so desperately to speak a language they need to believe once existed. But I do not see the breakdown of our language for parenting as a disaster. I see it as an opportunity and as ushering in a quite new kind of politics, fuelled by what people actually experience in their emotional and personal lives.

The politics of paternal warmth

I want to move on to discuss the ordinary physical warmth that fathers can communicate to their daughters and sons. This is my starting point for an exploration of the detail of the good-enough father of whatever sex. I think the detail is as important as the overall vision.

In all the completely justified concern over child sexual abuse, we have perhaps forgotten to say enough about the positive aspects of a father's physical warmth. In fact, I would go so far as to say that many conventional families have lacked this kind of experience, which can generate its own particularly pernicious brand of psychic pain. Any woman bringing up children alone or together with another woman is bound to be giving some thought already to what the positive outcomes of the provision of fatherly warmth would be. She will be doing this so as to decide whether or not to attempt to become the father of whatever sex and provide similar experiences leading to similar outcomes. She will be thinking about ways to do this.

Fatherly warmth leads to a form of recognition of his daughter as a female person in her own right, not simply as a little mother, not only as a creature tied into the image and role of mother. The sensitive and empathic break-up of an equation that woman equals mother has enormous sociopolitical implications as well as being important on a personal level. Many feminist writers have shown convincingly that the "reproduction of mothering" is terribly limiting for women. It ties a woman into the role of the one who looks after others, who responds and reacts to their needs, putting her own needs last, and not daring to risk disfavour and disapproval by expressing her assertiveness and demands. My idea is that fatherly recognition of the daughter as other than a mother can be seen as one key way in which women break out of the cycle of the reproduction of mothering (Chodorow, 1978). Then other pathways emerge: a spiritual path, a work path, a path that integrates her assertive side, a path of sexual expression (not necessarily heterosexual), maybe a path of celibacy. Crucially, there have to be pathways that are not man-oriented, that involve movement away from the father—for example, a path of solidarity and community with other women.

Women who are bringing up children alone can, by imagination and thought based on their sharing of experiences, send similar messages to their daughters. They can do this by understanding their daughter's evolving sexual potential as the most easily recognisable in a series of moves that takes her away from a mix-up or overlap with the mother. My stress on the sexual daughter is deliberate here. I am not saying mothers are not sexual. What I am saying is that a recognition of her daughter's evolving sexuality by a *woman* plays a part in turning that daughter away from a path in life that is completely circumscribed by the maternal role. To function as the father of whatever sex in this way may mean a woman who parents alone actually seeking out and accentuating what goes on in families around competition between parent and child of the same sex. If the woman who parents alone can communicate to her daughter that the daughter is a potential rival (in many diverse respects, not just oedipal rivalry) and can go on to communicate that this is not a bad thing, then she will be able to provide the kind of differentiation from the mother that the father's recognition, fuelled by mutual physical warmth between father and daughter, can provide. This would be a differentiation on an experiential level rather than an objectively measurable separation from the mother.

I will now return to the male father for a moment to say that it is timely for Western societies to address the habit of splitting perceptions of the male body into something either quite horribly abusive and violent (see Kuss & Harvey, 1987) or something meekly pretty, nice, hairless. Male bodies have potentials to do good as well as harm and we need to get a discussion going about *both* of these possibilities, far beyond the use of men's idealised bodies in advertising.

We should not forget that the communication of a positive physical warmth is pleasant and moving for both participants. The father gets something out of what I call "erotic playback" as well as the daughter. Nor should we forget that, once the initial equation woman equals mother is broken up, the outcome for a girl is unpredictable, also subject, for example, to her mother's behaviour in relation to her development. She may want and need to grow away from her father, away from the world of men in general, to seek out, work with, fall in love with, and raise children with other women. She will certainly have to negotiate the values, assumptions, and expectations of the society in which she lives.

My point is not that the father simply liberates the daughter or permits her to take up different psychosocial roles, including maternity if she desires it. No—the relationship of the daughter with the father of whatever sex has something to do with the plurality of differing psychosocial roles—the ways in which all those pathways I mentioned do or do not shake down for women into a workable blend of oneness and manyness. Who can doubt that this is already a key social issue for women—how to be more than one person at the same time while still managing to stay psychologically whole? There are now many mainstream books about superwoman or supermum and her balancing act (e.g., Gieve, 1989). So these ideas of mine about the father–daughter connection are not just of professional psychological interest (see Hewitt, 1993).

I will now discuss the part played by the father's physical warmth and erotic playback in relation to the son. For sons, a good-enough physical connection to the father helps to lead to the growth of what I argue should be called "homosociality" (after Sedgwick, 1985). The political implications of this are truly immense. What I am arguing here is that a certain kind of intimate father-son relating, prompted by positive physical warmth that is frankly expressed between them, inspires the new kinds of social organisation that Western societies need absolutely urgently just now. I am referring to a stress on community and on non-hierarchical organisation, which are just as valid modes of masculinity as the pecking order and the rat race. They are also modes of being that women may find more congenial than aping all the worst features of the male drive for success.

In these new visions of social organisation, men learn from other men just as they love them. Homosociality is illustrated by the ways in which the gay community has responded to AIDS, particularly at a time in the 1980s when AIDS was thought to be a problem only for homosexuals. Social and community innovations, such as "buddying" were seen then and can be seen now as referring to a particular kind of homoeroticised politics. In this kind of male relating, we have practical and inspiring political models for fathers and sons (as well as for brothers). Love between men, as between father and son, and even between brothers, can be seen as a kind of political practice or praxis. Notice the paradox: the group of men regarded by our society as the least "manly" have become, in my reframing of it, the pioneers, the frontiersmen, the new leaders in forging a way through a huge and hostile territory (see Edwards, 1990).

In this thinking about the good-enough father, I have come to see that a tremendous fear that the ordinary, devoted good-enough father will somehow be "homosexual" (see Hunter, 1992) is perhaps the most difficult obstacle to overcome. I suggest that Western societies have employed a fear and loathing of homosexuality as a cultural weapon to keep all men as a group tied into the role of provider in the family, the one who must therefore remain emotionally distant. The pay-off for men has been access to economic and political power, and I will return to this theme later in the chapter.

The virgin territory of homosocial father-son relations is a place in which the female father of whatever sex comes into *her* own and can function as a resource for her male co-fathers. Without undue idealisation, it seems likely that women know more about community and non-hierarchical organisation from the inside, as it were. It is clear that many women who parent alone have already considered how to make co-operation more attractive to their sons, rather than its being regarded as bland or, worst of all, non-manly. I have seen this going on in lone parent families on numerous occasions. The mother—I mean, of course, the father of whatever sex—using her undeniable power to reinforce and support an absence of hierarchy and unbendable rules, asking, even challenging her son to use his imagination as much as his biceps. And the sons respond to the challenge. They know at some level that being an old-style oppositional man, testing and testing the limits of authority, is only one way to be male. And it can be pretty boring. For sure, that kind of boundary-testing behaviour is not going to vanish overnight; it also has some positive aspects in that rules should be challenged and gathering new knowledge does involve breaking rules. But the father of whatever sex knows quite a lot already about working co-operatively—remember, in the old language, which has collapsed, she's a woman.

The politics of paternal aggression

So far, what I have been writing has been on the more erotic side of life—physical warmth and recognition of the daughter as other than mother, father–son togetherness as leading to reforms in how we conceive of society itself. What about aggression, an altogether more problematic theme, with an obsession about the elimination of criminal violence in society placed firmly at the back of people's minds by the media in many Western countries? Given such a Zeitgeist, it may be objected that I shall have to concede that only men can handle their sons' aggression.

It depends on what we mean by "handle" aggression. If we mean to eliminate aggression from the picture altogether, either by discipline that somehow magically works or by advocating a kind of stoicism in the face of frustration or adversity, then I would say that these might well be the hopelessly unachievable goals that a typical old-style male parent destined for a career in politics might aim for. But the question need not be couched in terms of how to handle, manage, discipline, do away with aggression: aggression cannot be eliminated from social process. For me, the task is rather to see how aggression might be kept moving and prevented from degenerating into the destructiveness that comes on to the scene when aggression gets stuck. Aggression is part of communicating. It is also a good and valid way of getting the attention of the other. The trouble is: Who is to say whether a particular piece of aggression is horridly destructive or constructively self-assertive? I return to these questions in my final section.

Exercise: I have developed an experiential way of looking at aggression that enables us to address this question of aggression getting stuck and turning into destructiveness. We can use the human body as a sort of index for aggression: there would be head aggression, which might take the form of a verbal onslaught; or chest aggression, exemplified by the ambivalence of the bear hug; or there's genital aggression—pornography, Don Juanism, or the materialistic sexual thrills of the tycoon; arm aggression suggests a whole range of images and acts—from pressing the button to striking a blow with a weapon to strangulation with bare hands; leg aggression is often practised by fathers—leg aggression means walking away, ducking the confrontation; anal aggression, stemming from the bottom, means enviously smearing the achievements of others, perhaps by snide comments—what those involved in encounter groups in the late 1960s used to call "coming out sideways".

My idea is that the relationship between the child and the father of whatever sex is the place in which movement between these various styles of aggression is worked on and developed, the main aim being to keep aggression fluid and moving through the various styles so as to avoid one style starting to predominate. When that happens, when one style does start to take over all the other styles, then you get the move from benevolent aggression to pure destructiveness.

But there's more to the communication of aggression between father and child than keeping several styles of aggression going at once. There is also the possibility of there being an element in fathering that can help to *transform* antisocial, sadistic, unrelated aggression into socially committed, self-assertive, related aggression. I see this transformation as taking place on the social level as well as in families.

I am particularly interested in how fathers work on these questions of aggression without knowing that they are doing it. For their sons, the goal seems to be to allow aggression its place in open and emotionally mobile relationships. For their daughters, the goal seems to be to validate and reinforce their capacity to challenge and fight with men. I think that a woman's personal capacity to confront the patriarchy stems to a certain extent from how her father played her aggressive response to him back to her.

What of aggression and the father of whatever sex? As far as women who parent alone are concerned, the main thing to think about in relation to the daughter concerns the need not to retreat into an all-female, nicey-nicey, sisterly alliance that would be spurious in its denial of aggression. I know from talking to lone parents how tempting it is for anyone who is isolated or who fears rejection to do this. Equally, many women who parent alone have simply had to come to terms with aggression in the family already. It is amazing that this point hasn't surfaced in the mainstream media. I wonder if it would be possible to go on to communicate to all lone parents of whatever sex that it is not only okay, but actually may often be a good thing, if they and their daughters fight. If the psychological professions were to speak of the need for women parenting alone to fight with their daughters, we would be changing the terms of debate about lone parent families and also posing a few questions for two parent families. For example, in two parent families, it is equally important that mothers communicate to their daughters that it is okay to challenge male authority—and it is supportive of the daughter, not disloyal and undermining of the father, for mothers to approve of such a challenge where it seems justified.

As far as the father of whatever sex and her son are concerned, I think that the observation about the need to avoid aggression getting stuck is important. There is always going to be tension and frustration in a family and this is always going to bear the possibility of aggression. But this can be reframed within the family from the earliest time as a part of relationship, not necessarily as something to be eliminated. In terms of actual parenting behaviour, I think that women who parent alone need to be reassured of what many know already: that it cannot be wrong in principle to engage in rough and tumble play with boys and that such play is bound to become a bit too real from time to time. It is not always a bad thing when events get a bit out of control—just look at the psychological damage done to people who grew up in tight, emotionally over-controlled families (father certainly there as a moral presence). What kind of training in handling aggression do such people get?

The days when male aggression was accepted in an uncomplicated way are over. That does not mean that the frequency of male violence has gone down. But cultural attitudes have become more intricate and difficult to decode (see Squire, 1994). The father of whatever sex derives some of her strength from these changes in cultural values—and maybe her contribution will make things change even more.

Can fathers change?

I have deliberately not taken an easy road concerning the father of whatever sex and how that father can be a good-enough father. I have not mentioned the fact that many children living in families headed by one parent do have contact with the other parent, or the ways in which women who parent alone can facilitate contact between their children and adult males, or the part male mentors might play in some families. These are pretty obvious points and they have often been made. But the battle of ideas has to be fought without recourse to a more palliative contribution if the stigmatisation of lone parent families by means of an idealisation of the father is to be halted.

If some readers cannot agree with me, if the idea of a father of whatever sex being good enough just goes against everything they believe in, I would ask merely that they note that it is *possible* to say it, it is *possible* to depict the father of whatever sex as a good-enough father, it is *possible* to challenge the assumption that only a male can do some of these things. I would urge such readers not to forget how many men do not or cannot do them before it is regarded as impossible for a women to do them.

Perhaps some readers have little problem with women doing the fathering but do not like the idea that fathers, or men in general, can change. In fact, fatherhood shows incredible cross-cultural variation (see Eleftheriadou, 1994) and changes over time; it is not something written in stone. There is one piece of empirical research that fascinates me. Everyone knows that fathers and mothers are said to play with children very differently. If they are videoed, the fathers are seen to be much more active, physical and so on, while the mothers are quieter, more reflective and protective. The picture seems logical and eternal ... well, if the play of fathers who, for whatever reason, have sole or primary care of children is videoed, *their* play resembles that of *mothers* (Raphael-Leff, 1991, pp. 372, 533). Fathers can change. Maybe men can change.

One way in which men are changing is that they are becoming more aware of a deal that they have made with Western societies. In this deal, the male child, at around four or five years old or even earlier, agrees to repudiate all that is soft, vulnerable, playful, maternal, "feminine", by hardening himself against these traits (see Phillips, 1993). In return, he gets special access to all the desire-fulfilling goodies that Western capitalism seems able to provide. Increasingly, and especially in mid-life, men are becoming aware that the deal was not altogether a good one from their point of view (Clay, 1989). Among many experiences which are denied them by the deal, the experience of being a hands-on, actively involved father of very small children is the one that is relevant for the argument here.

In my books, I have always urged caution in relation to men changing! The parallels that have been drawn between the so-called men's movement and the women's movement are fallacious because of the political reality of male possession of power and resources. Reference to the sobbing little boy inside every powerful man as "feminine" (e.g., Moore & Gillette, 1990) is one highly sexist false parallel that is drawn. And we should certainly listen to what the empirical social scientists tell us about the unchanging picture in most households with men not looking after children, not doing their share of the chores, and being responsible for most of the sexual and physical abuse that is perpetrated (see Croghan, 1991).

But something—what I have called the "aspirational atmosphere"—is changing. This is very hard to measure empirically, and the intuition of a depth psychologist sometimes does not pass muster when compared to "real" social science. What we can say is that if men are changing, if we are about to see good-enough fathers in larger numbers, then the very existence of male power takes on a new significance. The existence of male power means that, if changes are taking place in the world of men and fathers, there will be immense political and social effects in the not-too-distant future. This is almost the key background political issue of our times. It is certainly something mainstream politicians should attend to by paying heed to identity politics (see Butler, 1990). Gender issues are especially important for politics and for therapy because gender is something that sits midway between the outer world and the inner world. On the one hand, women are socio-economically disadvantaged compared with men and this can be measured. On the other hand, gender is a story of a most intimate and private kind that we tell ourselves about who we are; it is a story with many narrative rules that may change over time. So our subjective *and* our public lives are riddled with gender issues. Indeed, one way of understanding the unending wave of sex scandals in British and, indeed, world politics is to see them as highlighting how shaky and shifting are our present images of masculinity and how problematic we are finding it to work out what are and are not acceptable modes of behaviour for men.

However, when discussing male economic power or the psychological power of the father, we run a risk of lumping all men together. Taken as a whole, men certainly have power. But many black men, gay men, men who are physically challenged, men living in homelessness and poverty, men who have lost custody cases, young men dying in pointless wars or rotting in prison cells, and men whose countries have been invaded or occupied, might well dispute that they really do have power (see Dollimore, 1991).

Throughout the chapter, I have referred to lone parents knowing many things about good-enough fathering and doing them already. That does not remove the necessity to get ideas like these down on paper and inserted into a public debate. People living in lone parent families have become experts at living with the changes in gender role that are sweeping over the Western world. Could we reframe lone parents and their children as today's experts at coping with changes that threaten to drive everyone crazy by their depth and rapidity? There's an opportunity here as well as a crisis. The attack on lone parents has presented us with an opportunity to inject psychological realism and sensitivity into our politics, acknowledging that the old politics, which sought to leave out personal experience, is falling to pieces. People living in lone parent families are expert practitioners of this new kind of psychological politics. Government, the media, academics, and analysts like me should honour their expertise and try to learn from them.

Will analysts learn? For this to happen, a good deal of unlearning will have to take place.

Realising that the father himself is a culturally constructed creature of relationship leads to all kinds of rather exciting possibilities. If the father relation is always a product of two other relationships (the pair bond between a man and a woman, and the maternal bond between a mother and her child), then it is a constructed relationship, made in culture; that's why it cannot be approached via absolute definition; it is a situational and relative matter. If we can face this, then we will sense that a new judgement is required on our part towards what probably seems to many like hopelessly idealistic and utopian attempts to change the norms of father's role. I am saying that the father's role can change because written into the father's role is the refusal of an absolute definition of it. This refusal is made possible, not to put too fine a point on it, because of male power and freedom and because of the historical and cultural mutability of the father relation that I have just described. Hence, in one sense of the word, the only "archetypal" element in connection with the father is that there is no archetypal element in connection with the father. In full paradoxical form: the archetypal point about the father is that he is culturally constructed. To paraphrase Simone de Beauvoir (1947), he is one of those beings whose essence consists in having no essence—"*L'être dont l'être de n'être pas*" (p. 14).

But researching the psychoanalytic and psychotherapeutic literature, it is still hard to find many texts of paternal sexuality that depict its benevolent aspects as opposed to seizing on its undeniably malevolent aspects. To the contrary, in my vision of it, the father's body may turn out to resist censure and to contain a hidden sanctioning of the cultural diversity and political emancipation of others, particularly his children. It has become common to note the mobility, enfranchisement, and emancipation of men in contrast to the oppression and subordination of women. But very little has been said about the father's potential to carry a positive attitude towards the mobility, enfranchisement, and emancipation of others. It is certainly not something we can exhort or force fathers to do. In this chapter, I have been suggesting that images and experiences of paternal sexuality often carry a secret symbolism for social and political change. With the daughter, the treasure is to see her move beyond motherhood in her conception of being a woman. With the son, the treasure is to experience what non-hierarchical and collaborative ways of being can be like. For children of both sexes, regeneration and renewal stand alongside the far better known paternal symbolism of an oppressive, repressive, and static political order. This would be a far more radical contribution from depth psychology and psychoanalysis than merely seeing a penis as a useful weapon for beating back the mother.

But no one can make use of a text or testimony that tells of the father's progressive reinforcement of political and social change until there is an acknowledgement of the potential existence of such a text. Trying to avoid idealisation, such a text might be raised to a level of consciousness that allows for its entry into cultural discourse. The fact is, we still do not really know what fathers do. If we did, then we could get on with the business of finding out how much or how little of fathering has to do with maleness.

Fathering certainly has to do with children, and the next chapter is about "the child".

CHAPTER TEN

First catch your child

(With apologies to Mrs. Beeton, who began her recipe for jugged hare with the exhortation "First, catch your hare".)

In this chapter, I'm addressing three issues. First, who or what is the child that we have in mind when bemoaning the advent of what has been called "toxic childhood"? Second, can therapy really make a difference to whatever educational malaise Britain is currently suffering from? Third, is it possible that our educational debates and discussions of educational issues by politicians have become too "heady" and abstract, and could this imbalance be managed better by more of a focus on the body?

In search of the child

The child in question is, of course, a real person, and childhood is a genuine phase of life with real ups and downs, joys and sufferings. But there has always been something beyond the literal child that awakens when the image of the child arises in an individual or within a group. This imaginal child is something more than a recognition that there is a child in every adult. This child is the best known and most potent symbol of renewal, renaissance, and repair. It is nothing short of the divine (or very special) child, and we see this phenomenon in all cultures

141

and at all historical times—the Christ child is merely the majoritarian version in the West. If a culture loses contact with this collective image of the child, as ours may have, then it is in the deepest possible crisis.

Clients in therapy dream of babies and children at moments of change and at turning points in their lives. But the child of renewal is very vulnerable, and those same clients will perhaps also dream of the child being gobbled up by a monster or mistreated by abusive adults. I suggest that it is the paradox of divine power coupled with appalling vulnerability that is the essence of the child image. This is the mix that makes all our discussions about the literal, fleshy, actual child so hot, so divisive, and so emotionally draining. It is not just the sense of responsibility for the weak that drains, but also the sense that we are really on to something fulfilling needs that are as deep and complex as is imaginable.

So the image of the child makes our discussions of childhood harder than they might otherwise be. There's more to think of in the same vein. When we speak or write of childhood, we tend to project our adult worries and anxieties on to the image or icon of the child. So the child becomes the carrier of, the projection screen for, our adult angst. Please note: this is not the same as saying that adults are responsible for the problems faced by children. I am saying that the child in the adult mind is not only objectively a child, nor the adult's child bit—it is put into the adult's mind by the adult to do a job for an adult. Hence, all the evils that constitute toxic childhoods—the time problem, the lack of imaginative play, the obstacles to finding long-standing good-enough relationships—are contemporary adult problems writ large upon the personification we call the child. Is this abusive? Some might think so. What can be said confidently is that the child we think about today may be akin to the canary the miners used to take down the pit to check for gas. At the moment, the child is the diagnostic problem. In the 1980s and 1990s it was men who were the problem. Before that, in the 1950s, 1960s, and 1970s, women were the problem.

This observation leads me to the question often posed in therapy circles: Do adults really love children? The official answer is that we are ambivalent towards them, meaning that we both love and hate them. The hating bit is worth considering, for it brings up the question of whether or not adults can ever get over their envy of children. Envy is a very complex emotion because, though markedly negative, it usually conceals grudging, secret admiration. But envy often leads to profoundly destructive behaviour and so we have to face the possibility that we have created a crappy world for children because at some level we wanted to do it.

Envy has another element to it, which is even more relevant for debates on childhood that have an educational focus. Envy is the fuel of conformism. When we envy someone, we are often trying to cut them down to size, to our size, in what the Australians call the "tall-poppy syndrome", where the outstanding one has to be dealt with and forcibly reintegrated into the normal, the mass, the conventional.

A final point about this child we are trying to catch concerns our anxiety about ways we believe childhood to be a decisive era of personal development, controlling and causing all that we perceive in the adult personality. Here, therapists seem to divide into two camps. One group sees the events of early childhood as absolutely decisive for the individual's future, whether this is expressed in the language of attachment or in the terminology of the new "science" of affective neuroscience. So we had better worry a lot about childhood because what happens then is going to be so important for the future. And as parents are the ones who have to do the job of bringing up the children, it is parents who need to be educated, cajoled, bribed into good practices.

The problem with this is that no one really knows what good practices are. Fashions in parenting change. In the 1970s, a wonderful book entitled *For Her Own Good: 150 Years of the Experts' Advice to Women* (Ehrenreich & English, 1978) made this point with effortless impact. Over time, the experts of the day will contradict the experts of yesterday. Maybe it is a special example of the use of the child as a projection screen that I mentioned earlier.

Other therapists are less sure that the early years are as decisive as their colleagues say they are. This second group believes in the possibility of recovery from childhood difficulties (with or without therapy), and at any time in life. Some therapists believe that adversity and trauma can stimulate growth and development, that suffering brings its own gifts with it. This second group of therapists tends to welcome the idea that babies and children are individuals from conception onwards. Though marked by life, they are who they are, and we should be careful not to jump to conclusions about someone's life prospects based on recovery of facts that are, as often as not, very far from one single truth about a life.

Therapy thinking and educational practice

Contrary to what our critics splutter, therapists with an interest in public policy are not trying to put everyone on a couch. Rather, they want to use their knowledge base in a public way in the same manner that other professions—sociology economics, medicine—seek to. To illustrate what I have in mind, I'm going to take a few ideas from each of the three main schools of therapy and show how these inform what we might hope for from a teacher today. It seems to me important to take the ideas from all schools of therapy because, at the time of writing, there is a serious risk that the British Government will privilege one of them over the other in terms of public funding. I hope to show that it is not necessary to be an expert in the therapy field to understand how its ideas might turn out to be useful within education.

Psychoanalysis

Psychoanalysis is the oldest of these three schools of therapy, and its current focus is on the role of "relationality" in most aspects of life, including in learning. But for psychoanalysis, relationships are not only between persons: we also relate to a version of another person inside ourselves. So there is an anticipation of all kinds of distortions, and this is not something confined to the person who seeks therapeutic help—the practitioner is also in the same boat, full of her or his own subjective distortions with respect to the client and to much else. Teachers, too, bring their inner worlds to their relationships with their pupils. So a teacher might learn to ask herself or himself: "Do I really like this child?" "If not, why not? Is it something to do with me?" "Do I care?" "What in my own childhood has been awakened by this particular child or class of children?" In this way, to use a further term from psychoanalysis, education becomes a "third", something co-created between teacher and pupil or class.

Psychoanalysis also makes use of a definition of "thinking" that is far wider than the one most people use. What goes on behind our conscious knowledge is not only crazy or out of control, but is also quite sensible and "intelligent". That's why we sleep on problems, or, to be a little more positive, how creative ideas arise. They just do! Jung said there were two types of thinking—directed thinking, which is the kind most people are referring to when they use the word, and undirected thinking. Undirected thinking is sometimes called fantasy thinking or intuitive thinking, and in many ways it involves thinking in images or thinking through the body and its sensations.

The point is that learning does not only take place at the cognitive level but also at this other level of undirected, fantasy, intuitive thinking. The difficulty is that most educational practice does not explicitly recognise that this other level exists at all. The conditions for realising the potential of this second type of thinking are not, in principle, difficult to achieve. There needs to be a safe place, a relationship of trust, and the active encouragement of a passive approach to learning with great respect paid to the dreamy, fantastical, imaginative, and generally "pointless" sides of being. I think many readers will recognise what I am saying about the immensely creative power of undirected thinking but, for the most part, will not have seen this as a social and educational good.

Humanistic psychology

Humanistic psychology began as a reaction against psychoanalysis (and also against behaviourism, of which more in a moment). Generally speaking, humanistic approaches to therapy refer to the potential for growth and self-realisation that exists in everyone, no matter what their apparent circumstances. In its positive and optimistic outlook, humanistic psychology sometimes resembles a secular religion, though, as the name suggests, it is certainly not a religion. But sometimes, humanistic ideas do excite the derision that we have come to expect when religious ideas are introduced to public debates: too idealistic, out of touch with reality, won't work in practice, if only people were really as nice as that …

For educationalists, the tenets of humanistic therapy are extremely relevant. If one recalls the questions I imagined a teacher asking herself or himself on the basis of psychoanalytic ideas, the equivalent ones stemming from the humanistic field would be: "Can I find something good in this child?" "What is this child good at?" "What could this child teach me?" "Am I in fact expecting this child to fail (or misbehave or go crazy)?" There is a wealth of empirical evidence concerning the efficacy of optimism, and many people can track back in their lives to a time when someone in authority, not necessarily a parent but often a teacher, seemed to "believe" in them.

Cognitive behavioural therapy

Cognitive behavioural therapy is the third and last of the three main schools of contemporary psychotherapy. This is a structured approach to problems that rests on the idea that much mental and emotional distress, and many disturbing symptoms such as obsessions, compulsions, and phobias, are due to the acquisition of bad habits by faulty learning. Once these bad habits have been dissected and understood, the individual will be free of them.

In the educational context, the uses of therapy thinking derived from cognitive behaviour therapy are almost endless. I would like to single out the idea that much anxiety—which is generally agreed to interfere with learning—is the result of the acquisition of what seemed to be coping strategies that have, so to speak, gone sour. For example, a child who cannot concentrate may be understood as having stopped thinking about anything at all, lest she or he have to think about something horrid. Drifting off was a coping strategy that is, after some time, manifestly destructive and useless to the individual. Teachers could begin to make notes on this particular phenomenon, trying to ascertain what the mislearned coping strategy is, and helping the child to address the problems in a different and more productive way.

Reprise

Let me reprise what I have tried to achieve in this section of the chapter. I wanted to show how therapy thinking, not therapy itself, could contribute to how we understand the learning process in an educational setting. I took some ideas from each of the three main schools of therapy, and tried to demonstrate their utility to teachers. From psychoanalysis, I took the ideas that learning takes place within a two-way highly subjective and emotionally charged relationship and that there is more to thinking than meets the eye; from humanistic therapy, the idea that optimism works; from cognitive behaviour therapy, the idea that what was learned as yesterday's coping solution becomes today's diversionary problem.

Learning the body

This section makes use of work I did with the Personal, Social, and Health Education (PSHE) team at a small North London independent school covering the age range two to eight. Its roots are therefore highly practical, and actually involve attempts to align innovative practices with what the national curriculum requires for its foundation stage.

At my suggestion, this school opted to teach PSHE on a markedly bodily basis. So, for example, reproductive and sex education did not omit questions of desire and pleasure. Touch, mutual grooming of a simple kind, and the management of aggression were highlighted. Hygiene and self-care were, similarly, looked at in a more psychological way than is often the case. For example, it was proposed that children discuss the words they might use to express the nature, intensity, and duration of pain. This would include the more emotional side of pain as well as the obviously needed informational aspect.

One specific example of the use of an approach to PSHE derived from therapy thinking was to approach the senses through the imaginative conceit of being deprived of them. Not what we see, but what it is like not to see.

> Exercise: Look at something—then cover your eyes—what do you see and feel now?—and so on and so forth, through the senses.

In this way, the darker and more complex aspects of having a body are introduced at an early stage. This is a culturally congruent way of freeing children from the restrictions imposed on them in an age of anxiety and panic over every aspect of our corporeal existence.

CHAPTER ELEVEN

Jung and anti-Semitism: definitely not a therapy for politics*

Earlier in this book, I said I was both an enthusiast for the linkage of therapy thinking and politics—and also a sceptic. If I am a sceptic, one reason is the awful story of how Jung blundered into the political maelstrom of Germany in the 1930s. Maybe he had good intentions, maybe not. But I feel outlining some of the issues and my thoughts concerning them in this final chapter will helpfully (and hopefully) anchor this book.

Jung—for and against

Jung's activities and ideas have been the subject of intense criticism from the 1930s to the present day, but he has not lacked his ardent defenders. That defence has usually taken the form of testimony to the absence of anti-Semitism in his dealings with Jewish colleagues. Jung,

---

*Publication note: Readers who are familiar with my writings on Jung and anti-Semitism (in *The Political Psyche*) may not need to study again the cautionary tale that I told therein. This is a much shortened and revised version of that work, published originally in *The Jewish Quarterly* and greatly benefiting from their editorial input and feedback.

it has been affirmed, was particularly generous in support of those colleagues who were experiencing practical difficulties in the 1930s because of their Jewish origins, helping some to get out of Germany. As an analyst, Jung was apparently adept at putting patients in touch with their ethnic and religious antecedents. He claimed that severance of such links, with the consequent psychological strain, was a common and problematic feature for many sophisticated European Jews. Hence, from one perspective, it has been suggested, Jung's work may even be regarded as pro-Semitic. Such, at least, has been a large element in the conventional defence of Jung by his admirers. However, before coming to some conclusion concerning this defence, it is necessary to look at the relevant historical data.

In 1933 Jung took on the presidency of the General Medical Society for Psychotherapy. This was a professional body with members from several countries, but was primarily based in Germany and hence coming under Nazi control. Jung claimed that he took this post expressly to defend the rights of Jewish psychotherapists, and he altered the constitution of the GMSP so that it became a fully and formally international body. Membership was by means of national societies, with a special category of individual membership. Jews were already barred from membership in the German national society and so had to join as individuals. (To put this in context, it should be noted that Freud's books had been burnt, and he was officially banned in 1933.)

Jung was also editor of the *Zentralblatt*, the society's scientific journal. According to Jung, this was a strictly *pro forma* appointment, and he remained geographically (and presumably ideologically) distant from the editorial offices. He also maintained that he did not know of pro-Nazi statements of principles that were inserted in the *Zentralblatt* by Professor Goering (a cousin of the Reichsmarschall), who had been made president of the dominant German section.

Be that as it may, Jung's own editorials and articles in the *Zentralblatt*, extracts of which are quoted below, have also been a reason why he has been accused of pro-Nazi sympathies during this period. According to Geoffrey Cocks in *Psychotherapy in the Third Reich*, Jung's ideas had "official approval" and, as a result, "German psychotherapists did all they could to link Jung's name to their own activities" (Cocks, 1985, p. 129). Jung's work was in fact cited by German racial theoreticians and appeared in official Nazi bibliographies of the period.

In an interview on Radio Berlin in 1933, Jung stated:

As Hitler said recently, the leader must be able to be alone and must have the courage to go his own way. But if he doesn't know himself, how is he to lead others? That is why the true leader is always one who has the courage to be himself, and can look not only others in the eye but above all himself. ... Every movement culminates organically in a leader, who embodies in his whole being the meaning and purpose of the popular movement. (Jung, 1933a, pp. 64–65)

And in his paper, "The state of psychotherapy today" (1934a, para 354), Jung wrote:

Freud ... did not understand the Germanic psyche any more than did his Germanic followers. Has the formidable phenomenon of National Socialism, on which the whole world gazes with astonishment, taught them better? Where was that unparalleled tension and energy while as yet no National Socialism existed? Deep in the Germanic psyche, in a pit that is anything but a garbage-bin of unrealizable infantile wishes and unresolved family resentments.

In the same paragraph, in a passage which clarifies the somewhat cryptic language above, Jung asserted (about Jews): "The 'Aryan' unconscious has a higher potential than the Jewish." And: "The Jew who is something of a nomad has never yet created a cultural form of his own and as far as we can see never will, since all his instincts and talents require a more or less civilized nation to act as host for their development" (para 353). And: "The Jews have this peculiarity in common with women; being physically weaker, they have to aim at the chinks in the armour of their adversary" (para 353). Jung went on to warn against "apply[ing] Jewish categories ... indiscriminately to Germanic and Slavic Christendom" (para 354).

A similar observation occurs in a footnote to the *Two Essays on Analytical Psychology*, first published in 1928 and republished in 1935: "[I]t is a quite unpardonable mistake to accept the conclusions of a Jewish psychology as generally valid" (1928a, para 240n).

In a *Zentralblatt* editorial he wrote that "[t]he differences which actually do exist between Germanic and Jewish psychology and which have been long known to every intelligent person are no longer to be glossed over" (1933b, para 1014). In a letter to his pupil Wolfgang Kranefeldt written in 1934, Jung wrote:

As is known, one cannot do anything against stupidity, but in this instance the Aryan people can point out that, with Freud and Adler, specifically Jewish points of view are publicly preached, and as can be proved likewise, points of view that have an essentially corrosive character. If the proclamation of this Jewish gospel is agreeable to the government, then so be it. Otherwise there is also the possibility that this would not be agreeable to the government. (Jung, 1977, p. 377)

Earlier, in 1918, Jung had written that the Jew "is badly at a loss for that quality in man which roots him to the earth and draws new strength from below. This chthonic quality is found in dangerous concentration in the Germanic peoples ... The Jew has too little of this quality—where has he his own earth underfoot?" (1918, para 18).

In his "Rejoinder to Dr. Bally" (1934b), who had Jung to task over some of these remarks, Jung wrote: "I must confess my total inability to understand why it should be a crime to speak of 'Jewish' psychology" (para 1027). Jung also asserts that "psychological differences obtain between all nations and races" (para 1029).

Omissions

I know my readers will not be expecting something comprehensive in a short study, but I still want to say a few words about what is *not* covered so that it is clear the omission is deliberate. I do not make much of psychobiography, of the facts of Jung's inner and outer life, his dreams, his father-complex, the scars of the break with Freud, his ambition, his shadow problem, his Swiss bourgeois mentality, and so forth. Nor do I devote much space to personal testimonies that show that Jung could not have been anti-Semitic and that he had a positive attitude to Jews and helped many achieve a relationship with their Jewishness for the first time. For a while, I worried that these omissions—that is, Jung's psychopathology and the evidence of people who knew him, neither of which should be entirely ignored— added up to a failure of feeling on my part. But gradually I have come to see that the true failure of feeling is found when the personal dimension is given too much weight or used to close an awkward issue once and for all.

The heart of the matter

What I *do* ask is whether there is something in the deep, fundamental structure of Jung's thought, in its heart or essence, that made it inevitable that he would develop a kind of anti-Semitism. When Jung writes about the Jews and Jewish psychology, is there something in his whole take or attitude that just had to lead to anti-Semitism? Is there something to worry about?

My brief answer, in contradistinction to that of many other leading Jungian analysts, is yes and my hope is that by exploring the matter as deeply as we can, a form of reparation will ensue. I believe that many strengths and subtleties of analytical psychology are being lost—not just because of the alleged Nazi collaboration and anti-Semitism, but also because of the evident inability of many Jungians to react to such charges in an intelligent, humane way. This permits the Freudian establishment, academia, and the rest of the civilised world, to continue to ignore the pioneering nature of Jung's contributions, and hence the work of post-Jungian analytical psychologists.

I am going to start in the middle of things, with Adolf Hitler and his ideas about the Jews. It is far too general and facile to see Hitler's theorising about the Jews solely as racist. There is also a comprehensive political and historical theory, and it is hard to disentangle the racial and political ideas. The political dogma certainly employs a racial viewpoint, but Hitler's racism also has a political format, one that uses a *nationalistic* vocabulary and focuses on the idea of the nation.

The modern idea of nation stems from the late eighteenth and early nineteenth centuries. The idea gradually arose that nationality was a natural possession of everyone and that a person could participate in civic and political life only as part of a nation. Just as political allegiance had hitherto not been determined by nationality, so civilisation was not previously regarded as nationally defined. During the Middle Ages, civilisation defined itself religiously and, in the Renaissance and Enlightenment periods, the classical cultures of Greece and Rome became the yardsticks. When civilisation started to be defined on the basis of nationality, it was felt for the first time that people should be educated in their own mother tongue, not in the language of other civilisations. Poets and scholars began to emphasise cultural nationalism. They reformed the national languages, elevating them to literary status and delved deep into the traditional past. The modern nation-state, with its central administration facilitated by rapid communication, is different from previous forms of political organisations.

Hitler regarded all history as consisting of struggles between competing nations for living space and, eventually, for world domination. The Jews, according to Hitler, are a nation and participate in these struggles, but their goal, quite directly and in the first instance, is world domination. This is because the Jews do not start off with possession of living space, of an identifiable, geographical locality; it has to be the world or nothing. In fact, for Hitler, the aim of the Jews is really "de-nationalization, the inter-bastardization of other nations" (quoted in Graham, 1984, p. 94). The Jewish nation achieves its goal of world domination by denationalising existing states from within and imposing a homogeneous "Jewish" character on them by its international capitalism and its equally international communism. So, in Hitler's thinking, there is a struggle between wholesome nationhood and its corrupting enemy, the Jews (see Haffner, 1979).

Jung, too, was interested in the idea of the nation, and he makes innumerable references (for example, in Jung, 1918, para 18) to "the psychology of the nation" and to the influence of a person's national background. He goes on to write that "the soil of every country holds [a] mystery. ... There is a relationship of body to earth." This culminates in the assertion that the skull and pelvis measurements of second-generation American immigrants were becoming "indianized". It can be seen that, even in such offensive craziness, Jung was not thinking along racial lines, for the immigrants from Europe and the indigenous Indians come from different races. No, living in America, living on *American soil*, being part of the American nation, these are what exert profound physiological and psychological effects. "The foreign land assimilates its conqueror", says Jung (1931, para 103), and his argument is not based on race but on earth and culture as the matrix from which we evolve. Earth plus culture equals nation.

However, at the moment we introduce the idea of nation, depth psychology just cannot remain untrammelled or uncontaminated by economic, social, political, and historical factors. For nation is an economic, social, political, and historical construct—and a relatively modern one at that. For example, the German nation, as a recognisable cultural and political phenomenon, did not exist before the rise of Prussia at the end of the eighteenth century (Khon, 1967). If we analyse German nationalism (or any other nationalism), we find that there is much more involved than emphasis on the geographical unit. We find some kind of ethical principle, or at least ethical expression, and this is usually couched in comparative (and selfcongratulatory) terms: our soldiers are the bravest and most moral, the quality of our family life is the finest, we have special rights, we have special responsibilities, we have a unique relationship to higher forces, our apple pie is the greatest, our upper lip the stiffest. In other words, nationalism always involves a form of psychological expression and self-characterisation, and therefore nationalism requires the services of psychologists.

It is my contention that, in C. G. Jung, nationalism found its psychologist. But in his role as a psychologist of nationhood, his role as a psychologist who lends his authority to nationalism, Jung's panpsychism (his phrase) ran riot. This refers to the tendency to see all outer events in terms of inner dynamics, and it led Jung to claim that the nation is just a personified concept that corresponds in reality only to a specific nuance of the individual psyche. "[The nation] is nothing but an inborn character ... Thus in many ways it is an advantage to have been imprinted with the English national character in one's cradle. You can then travel in the most god-forsaken countries and when anybody asks, 'Are you a foreigner?' you can answer, 'No, I am English'" (Jung, 1928b, para 921).

But, in spite of the humour, there is no evidence that Jung's approach to the concept of nation is fundamentally metaphorical or mythological—he means what he says.

Jung and Hitler

Let me draw some conclusions from the above. First, a crucial aspect of Hitler's thinking is that the Jews represent a threat to the inevitable and healthy struggle of different nations for world domination. Second, Jung's view is that each nation has a different and identifiable national psychology, that is, in some mysterious manner, an innate factor. At first sight, juxtaposing these two points of view might seem innocuous, or pointless, or even distasteful in itself. It is certainly not my intention to make a straightforward *comparison* of Hitler and Jung. But if we go on to explore the place of the Jews in Jung's mental ecology, to find out where they are situated in his view of the world, then the juxtaposition of the two points of view takes on a far more profound significance. For my aim is to see whether there is anything in the essence of Jung's thought, anything in its underlying structure and assumptions, that must lead him into the kind of anti-Semitism we are concerned with here.

My perception is that the ideas of nation and of national difference form a hinge between Jung's thinking and that of Hitler. For, as a psychologist of nations, Jung too would feel threatened by the Jews, this strange so-called nation without a land. Jung, too, would feel threatened by the Jews, this strange nation without cultural forms—that is, without *national* cultural forms—of its own, and hence, in Jung's words of 1934, requiring a "nation to act as host" (1934a, para 353). What threatens Jung, in particular, can be illuminated by enquiring closely into what he meant when he writes, as he often does, of "Jewish psychology". His use of the term is dramatically inconsistent.

There is a Jewish psychology, meaning the psychological characteristics, prejudices, and assumptions of a "typical" Jewish person. Jung argues that everybody is affected by their background and this leads to all kinds of prejudices and assumptions—"[e]very child knows that differences exist" (1934b, para 1029). One can agree or disagree with Jung's various statements about the typical Jew, but there is a second use by Jung of this term "Jewish psychology". It has another and more provocative implication. Here, he is referring to systems of psychology developed by Jews such as Freud and Adler, systems that claim universal applicability and truth. Such a psychology is a "levelling psychology" (Jung's words) in that it undermines the idea that there are psychological differences between groups of peoples such as nations (ibid.). Such a psychology is wrong to apply "Jewish categories ... indiscriminately" (1934a, para 354) and, as noted above, Jung states that one should not make the "unpardonable mistake [of] accept[ing] the conclusion of a Jewish psychology as generally valid" (1928a, para 240n).

Jung is saying that Jewish psychoanalysis attacks the idea of psychological differences between nations. Jewish psychoanalysis therefore occupies a place in Jung's mind analogous to the place occupied in Hitler's mind by Jewish international capitalism and Jewish international communism. The great fears are, respectively, "levelling" and "denationalizing". Jung and Hitler do not say exactly the same things about the Jews, of course, but the levelling aim of Jewish psychology and the denationalising aim of Jewish political and economic activity represents a similar kind of threat to each of them. So each develops a similar kind of obsession. For Hitler, this takes the form of an obsession with a Jewish "spirit", functioning as a pestilential bacillus, undermining the very idea of nation. For Jung, this takes the form of an obsession with a Jewish psychology, capable of being imposed on all other ethnic and national psychologies, bringing them all down to the same level.

Learnings and hopes

Since doing the research that led to these ideas, my hope has been that all analytical psychologists would work together on what these reflections might mean for their common humanity, their intellectual integrity and their identity as Jungian analysts. I believe that, via the issuance of public apologies and a great deal of archival research, the response from the Jungian analytical community—notably in Germany—has been more than satisfactory. As far as the future is concerned, I believe it would help if they (and others within psychotherapy) were to cease expanding the national boundaries of the psychological kingdom and try to work co-operatively with their colleagues in the social sciences. This means stopping the abuse of authority in advancing definitions of the typical innate psychology of this or that group—Jews, Germans, African-Americans, homosexuals, women. We should think seriously of abandoning Jung's method here.

What he did was to assemble lists of characteristics, taken as inborn, and use the lists to make a definition: definition of Jew, definition of German, it is exactly the same method that he used to define the psychological attributes of the two sexes. The emphasis is upon what a Jew *is*, not upon what being a Jew *is like*. The emphasis is on defining or predefining differences, but not on the experience of living out of difference. Just as with the sexes, we find Jung importing his ethos of complementarity so that any two opposite lists combined produce an absolutely wonderful-sounding wholeness. In Jung's writing, Jew and German seem to constitute two halves of a whole: rational, sophisticated, erudite city-dweller complementing irrational, energetic, earthy peasant-warrior. If one were to abandon Jung's method, then one might be able to revalue what he was trying to do. For, make no mistake about it, alongside the many problems with Jung's ideas about nation, race, and religion, there are also the seeds of a useful approach to difference. Even if Jung's method and ideology are suspect, his intuition of the importance of exploring difference remains intact. We can preserve a connection to Jung's intuition of the importance of difference but unhindered by excessive dependence on complementarity.

Then analysts and therapists could expressly ally themselves to so-called marginal or minority groups. They could contribute their limited but profound expertise to the achievement of the goals of such groups. The only thing therapists are good at is getting people to experience and express consciously what they implicitly know but have not yet thought or felt—what I have been calling the more-than personal in this book. Therapists could employ their skills and their capacity to work with the inexpressible in an exploration of the psychological experience of being a Jew, German, African-American, homosexual, woman, man. They could assist in getting behind the defensive stereotypes imposed by a threatened dominant culture as they probe the nature of difference itself. It is truly subversive work, breaking the modern veto on the discussion of national and racial difference. But it has to be done.

It is crucial that what differences there are between nations or between races or between classes or between sexes are not predefined. The therapist is not an authority or teacher who has a priori knowledge of the psychological implications of the client's ethnic and cultural background. Rather, the therapist is a mediator who enables the client to experience and express his or her own difference. Such a therapist can revalue and support Jung's impassioned rejection of the imposition of the psychology of one group upon another. Jungians in particular have had some reparation to make and have much to offer a general therapy project in relation to political processes.

REFERENCES

Adams, M. V. (1996). *The Multicultural Imagination: "Race", Color, and the Unconscious*. London: Routledge.

Altman, N. (1995). *The Analyst in the Inner City: Race, Class, and Culture Through a Psychoanalytic Lens*. Hillsdale, NJ: Analytic Press.

Atwood, M. (1972a). *Surfacing*. London: Virago.

Atwood, M. (1972b). *Survival: A Thematic Guide to Canadian Literature*. Toronto: Anansi Press.

Barker, M. (2004). This is my partner and this is my ... partner's partner: Constructing a polyamorous identity in a monogamous world. *Journal of Constructivist Psychology, 18*: 75–88.

Beck, U., & Beck-Gernsheim, E. (2002). *Individualization: Institutionalized Individualism and its Social and Political Consequences*. London: Sage.

Beckett, S. (1983). *Worstward Ho*. London: Faber, 2009.

Benjamin, J. (1988). *The Bonds of Love: Psychoanalysis, Feminism and the Problem of Domination*. New York: Pantheon.

Bersani, L. (1987). Is the rectum a grave? *October, 43*: 197–222.

Boff, L. (1988). *When Theology Listens to the Poor*. San Francisco, CA: Harper & Row.

Boyarin, D. (1993). *Carnal Israel: Reading Sex in Talmudic Culture*. Berkeley, CA: University of California Press.

Brecht, B. (1947). *The Life of Galileo*. London: Methuen.

159

Buber, M. (1957). *Tales of the Hasidism.* New York: Schocken.

Butler, J. (1990). *Gender Trouble: Feminism and the Subversion of Identity.* London: Routledge.

Camus, A. (1951). *The Rebel* (Trans. J. Laredo). London: Hamish Hamilton, 1953.

Chodorow, N. (1978). *The Reproduction of Mothering: Psychoanalysis and the Sociology of Gender.* Los Angeles, CA: University of California Press.

Clay, J. (1989). *Men at Midlife.* London: Sidgwick & Jackson.

Cocks, G. (1985). *Psychotherapy in the Third Reich.* London: Oxford University Press.

Croghan, R. (1991). First-time mothers: Accounts of inequality in the division of labour. *Feminism & Psychology, 1*: 221–246.

Cushman, P. (1995). *Constructing the Self, Constructing America.* Reading, MA: Addision-Wesley.

Davies, D., & Neal, C. (2000). *Therapeutic Perspectives on Working with Lesbian, Gay and Bisexual Clients.* Buckingham: Open University Press.

de Beauvoir, S. (1947). *Pour une morale de l'ambiguïté.* Paris: Gallimard.

Dimen, M. (1994). Money, love, and hate: Contradiction and paradox in psychoanalysis. *Psychoanalytic Dialogues, 4*: 69–100.

Dollimore, J. (1991). *Sexual Dissidence: Augustine to Wilde, Freud to Foucault.* Oxford: Oxford University Press.

du Plessix Gray, F. (1972). Introduction. In: M. Atwood, *Surfacing.* London: Virago.

Durkheim, E. (1893). *The Division of Labor in Society* (Trans. L. A. Coser). New York: Free Press, 1997.

Dylan, B. (1965). Song: *Love Minus Zero, No Limit.* Warner Bros. Read more: http://www.bobdylan.com/us/songs/love-minus-zero-no-limit#ixzz3YvSMisNr

Edwards, T. (1990). Beyond sex and gender: Masculinity, homosexuality and social theory. In: J. Hearn & D. Morgan (Eds.), *Men, Masculinities and Social Theory* (pp. 102–129). London: Unwin & Hyman.

Ehrenreich, B., & English, D. (1978). *For Her Own Good: 150 years of the Experts' Advice to Women.* New York: Bantam.

Eichenbaum, L., & Orbach, S. (1982). *Outside In ... Inside Out. Women's Psychology: A Feminist Psychoanalytic Approach.* Harmondsworth: Penguin.

Eleftheriadou, Z. (1994). *Transcultural Counselling.* London: Central Book Publications.

Eliot, T. S. (1943). *Four Quartets.* London: Faber.

Engels, F. (1884). *Origin of the Family: Private Property and the State.* New York: International Publishers, 1972.

Ficowski, J. (1979). Untitled poem (Trans. K Bosley). In: H. Shiff (Ed.), *Holocaust Poetry.* New York: St Martin's Press, 1995.

Fisher, D. (2007). Classical psychoanalysis, politics and social engagement in the era between the wars: Reflections on the free clinics. *Psychoanalysis and History, 9*: 237–250.

Foster, R., Moskowitz, M., & Javier, R. (1996). *Reaching Across Boundaries of Culture and Class: Widening the Scope of Psychotherapy.* Northvale, NJ: Jason Aronson.

Foucault, M. (1976). *The History of Sexuality. Volume 1: An Introduction.* London: Allen Lane, 1979.

Freud, S. (1905). *Three Essays on the Theory of Sexuality. S. E., 7.* London: Hogarth.

Freud, S. (1917). Mourning and melancholia. *S. E., 14.* London: Hogarth.

Freud, S. (1930). *Civilization and its Discontents. S. E., 21.* London: Hogarth.

Freud, S. (1933). *New Introductory Lectures on Psycho-Analysis. S. E., 22.* London: Hogarth.

Giddens, A. (1991). *Modernity and Self-Identity: Self and Society in the Late Modern Age.* Stanford, CA: Stanford University Press.

Gieve, K. (1989). *Balancing Acts: On Being a Mother.* London: Virago.

Goldberg, G. S., & Kremen, E. (Eds.) (1991). *The Feminization of Poverty: Only in America?* Westport, CT: Greenwood Press.

Gordon, R. (1987). Masochism: the shadow side of the archetypal need to venerate and worship. In: A. Samuels (Ed.), *Psychopathology: Contemporary Jungian Perspectives* (pp. 237–254). London: Karnac, 1989.

Goss, R. (2004). Proleptic sexual love: God's promiscuity reflected in Christian polyamory. *Theology and Sexuality, 11*: 52–63.

Graham, S. (1984). *Hitler, Germans and the "Jewish Question".* Princeton, NJ: Princeton University Press.

Gross, O. (1913a). Zur Uberwinding der kulturellen Krise. Die Aktion 1913a; III.Jahr: Cols. 384–387.

Gross, O. (1913b). Anmerkungen zu einer meuen Ethik. Die Aktion 1913b; III.Jahr: Cols. 1141–1143.

Haffner, S. (1979). *The Meaning of Hitler, Hitler's Uses of Power: His Successes and Failures.* New York: Basic Books.

Hemingway, E. (1941). *For Whom the Bell Tolls.* London: Arrow, 1994.

Heuer, G. (2001). Jung's twin brother: Otto Gross and Carl Gustav Jung. *Journal of Analytical Psychology, 46*: 655–688.

Hewitt, P. (1993). *About Time: The Revolution in Work and Family Life.* London: Rivers Oram Press.

Hillman, J., & Ventura, M. (1992). *We've Had a Hundred Years of Psychotherapy and the World's Getting Worse.* San Francisco, CA: Harper Collins.

Hinshelwood, R. D. (1989). *A Dictionary of Kleinian Thought.* London: Free Association Books.

Hoffman, K., & Kaplinsky, R. (1988). *Driving Force: The Global Restructuring of Technology, Labor, and Investment in the Automobile and Components Industries.* Boulder, CO: Westview Press.

Hunter, A. (1992). Same door, different closet: A heterosexual sissy's coming-out party. *Feminism & Psychology, 2:* 367–386.

Huysmans, J. -K. (1884). *Against Nature (À Rebours)* (Trans. R. Baldick). Harmondsworth: Penguin, 1959.

Jeffreys, S. (1990). *Anticlimax: A Feminist Perspective on the Sexual Revolution.* New York: New York University Press.

Except where indicated, references to Jung's *Collected Works* (CW) are by volume number in the references and by paragraph number in the text. Edited by H. Read, M. Fordham, G. Adler, and W. McGuire, translated in the main by R. Hull. London: Routledge & Kegan Paul.

Jung, C. G. (1916). Adaptation, individuation, collectivity. *CW18.*

Jung, C.G. (1918). The role of the unconscious. *CW10.*

Jung, C. G. (1921). Definitions. *CW6.*

Jung, C. G. (1928a). *Two Essays on Analytical Psychology. CW7.*

Jung, C. G. (1928b). The Swiss line in the European spectrum. *CW10.*

Jung, C. G. (1931). Mind and earth. *CW10.*

Jung, C. G. (1933a). An interview on Radio Berlin. In: W. McGuire & R. F. C. Hull (Eds.), *C. G. Jung Speaking: Interviews and Encounters* (pp. 59–66). London: Thames & Hudson, 1978.

Jung, C. G. (1933b). Editorial: *Zentralblatt* VI. *CW10.*

Jung, C. G. (1934a). The state of psychotherapy today. *CW10.*

Jung, C. G. (1934b). Rejoinder to Dr. Bally. *CW10.*

Jung, C. G. (1947). On the nature of the psyche. *CW8.*

Jung, C.G. (1952). Comments on a doctoral thesis. In: W. McGuire & R. F. C. Hull (Eds.), *C. G. Jung Speaking: Interviews and Encounters* (pp. 205–218). London: Thames & Hudson, 1978.

Jung, C. G. (1953). The relations between the ego and the unconscious. *CW7.*

Jung, C. G. (1957). The undiscovered self. *CW10.*

Jung, C. G. (1961). Letter to Bill W. In: *C. G. Jung Letters Volume 2* (Ed. G. Adler in collaboration with Aniela Jaffe). London: Routledge, 1973.

Jung, C. G. (1963). *Memories, Dreams, Reflections.* London: Collins.

Jung, C. G. (1977). Letter to Wolgang Kranefeldt, 9 February 1934, quoted by Mortimer Ostow in a letter to the editor. *International Review of Psycho-Analysis, 4:* 377.

Jung, C. G. (2009). *The Red Book: Liber Novus* (Ed. S. Shamdasani). New York: W. W. Norton.

Kahr, B. (2007). *Sex and the Psyche.* London: Allen Lane.

Kaplinsky, R. (1990). *The Economies of Small*. London: Intermediate Technology Press.

Kareem, J., & Littlewood, R. (Eds.) (1992). *Intercultural Therapy: Themes, Interpretations and Practice*. Oxford: Blackwell Scientific Publications.

Keynes, J. M. (1930). Economic possibilities for our grandchildren. In: J. M. Keynes, *Essays in Persuasion* (pp. 358–373). New York: Norton, 1963.

Keynes, J. M. (1936). *The General Theory of Employment, Interest and Money*. London: Macmillan.

Kohn, H. (1967). *The Idea of Nationalism: A Study in its Origins and Background*. Oxford: OUP.

Kuss, M., & Harvey, M. (1987). *The Rape Victim: Clinical and Community Approaches to Treatment*. Lexington, MA: Stephen Greene Press.

Lawrence, D. H. (1913). *Sons and Lovers*. Cambridge: Cambridge University Press, 1992.

Layton, L. (2013). Dialectical constructivism in historical context: Expertise and the subject of late modernity. *Psychoanalytic Dialogues, 23*: 126–149.

Layton, L., Hollander, N., & Gutwill, S. (2006). *Psychoanalysis, Class and Politics: Encounters in the Clinical Setting*. London: Routledge.

Leone, S. (1966). *The Good, the Bad and the Ugly* [Film]. Italy.

Levinas, E. (1995). *Alterity and Transcendence* (Trans. M. B. Smith). New York: Columbia University Press, 1999.

Luepnitz, D. A. (1988). *The Family Interpreted: Psychoanalysis, Feminism, and Family Therapy*. New York: Basic Books.

Magee, M., & Miller, D. C. (1997). *Lesbian Lives: Psychoanalytic Narratives Old and New*. Hillsdale, NJ: Analytic Press.

Miedzian, M. (1992). *Boys Will Be Boys: Breaking the Link Between Masculinity and Violence*. London: Virago.

Millet, C. (2001). *The Sexual Life of Catherine M*. London: Corgi, 2003.

Milton, J. (1667). *Paradise Lost*. Harmondsworth: Penguin, 2003.

Moore, R., & Gillette, D. (1990). *King, Warrior, Magician, Lover: Rediscovering the Archetypes of the Mature Masculine*. San Francisco, CA: Harper.

Murray, C. (1990). Underclass. In: D. Anderson & G. Dawson (Eds.), *Family Portraits*. London: Social Affairs Unit.

Musil, D. (1990). *Precision and Soul: Essays and Addresses of Robert Musil* (Ed. & trans. B. Pike & D. S Lufts). Chicago, IL: Chicago University Press.

Neumann, E. (1954). *The Origins and History of Consciousness*. London: Routledge & Kegan Paul, 1964.

O'Connor, J., Mumford, M., Clifton, T., Gessner, T., & Connelly, M. S. (1995). Charismatic leaders and destructiveness: An historiometric study. *The Leadership Quarterly, 6*: 529–555.

Okri, B. (1999). *Mental Fight*. London: Faber.

Orbach, S. (2009). *Bodies*. London: Profile.

Orwell, G. (1949). *1984*. London: Penguin.

Owen, W. (1916). *War Poems*. London: Faber.

Péguy, C. (1910). *Notre jeunesse*. Paris: Gallimard, 1993.

Phillips, A. (1993). *The Trouble with Boys: Parenting the Men of the Future*. London: Pandora.

Pickett, K., & Wilkinson, R. (2009). *The Spirit Level: Why More Equal Societies Almost Always Do Better*. London: Allen Lane.

Progoff, I. (1952). *Jung's Psychology and its Social Meaning*. New York: Julian Press.

Qualls-Corbett, N. (1987). *The Sacred Prostitute: Eternal Aspects of the Feminine*. Toronto: Inner City Books.

Raphael-Leff, J. (1991). *Psychological Processes of Childbearing*. London: Chapman & Hall.

Reich, W. (1927). *The Function of the Orgasm*. New York: Orgone Institute Press, 1942.

Richards, B. (Ed.) (1984). *Capitalism and Infancy: Essays on Psychoanalysis and Politics*. London: Free Association Books.

Ricoeur, P. (1967). *The Symbolism of Evil*. New York: Harper & Row.

Rivière, J. (1929). Womanliness as a masquerade. *International Journal of Psychoanalysis, 10*: 303–313.

Rose, N. (1989). *Governing the Soul: The Shaping of the Private Self*. London: Free Association Books.

Roth, P. (2001). *The Dying Animal*. London: Vintage, 2006.

Rumi, (2006). *Collected Poems*. Berlin: Shardar Press.

Rust, M. -J., & Totton, N. (2012). *Vital Signs: Psychological Responses to Ecological Crisis*. London: Karnac.

Samuels, A. (1985). *Jung and the Post-Jungians*. London: Routledge.

Samuels, A. (Ed.) (1986). *The Father: Contemporary Jungian Perspectives*. New York: Guilford Press.

Samuels, A. (1989). *The Plural Psyche: Personality, Morality and the Father*. London: Routledge.

Samuels, A. (1993). *The Political Psyche*. London: Routledge.

Samuels, A. (1996). From sexual misconduct to social justice. *Psychoanalytic Dialogues, 6*: 295–321.

Samuels, A. (1999). Working directly with political, social and cultural material in the therapy session. In: J. Lees (Ed.), *Clinical Counselling in Context*. London: Routledge.

Samuels, A. (2001). *Politics on the Couch: Citizenship and the Internal Life*. London: Karnac.

Samuels, A. (2002). The hidden politics of healing: Foreign dimensions of domestic practice. *American Imago, 59*: 459–482.

Samuels, A. (2004). A new anatomy of spirituality: Clinical and political demands the psychotherapist cannot ignore. *Psychotherapy and Politics International, 2*: 201–211.

Samuels, A. (2006). Socially responsible roles of professional ethics: Inclusivity, psychotherapy and "the protection of the public". *International Review of Sociology, 16*: 175–190.

Samuels, A. (2014). Shadows of the relational. In: D. Loewenthal & A. Samuels (Eds.), *Relational Psychotherapy, Psychoanalysis and Counselling* (pp. 184–192). London: Routledge.

Searles, H. (1973). Violence in schizophrenia. In: *Countertransference and Related Subjects: Selected Papers*. New York: International Universities Press, 1999.

Seccombe, W. (1993). *Weathering the Storm: The History of Working Class Families*. London: Verso.

Sedgwick, E. K. (1985). *Between Men: English Literature and Male Homosocial Desire*. New York: Columbia University Press.

Seeger, P. (1955). Where have all the flowers gone. *Sing Out, 11*: 4–5.

Seidler, V. (2007). *Jewish Philosophy and Western Culture: A Modern Introduction*. London: Tauris.

Sen, A. (1989). Women's survival as a development problem. *Bulletin of the American Academy of Arts and Sciences, 2*: 14–29.

Shamdasani, S. (2003). *Jung and the Making of Modern Psychology: The Dream of a Science*. Cambridge: Cambridge University Press.

Shorter, B. (1995). *Susceptible to the Sacred*. London: Routledge.

Singer, T., & Kimbles, S. L. (Eds.) (2004). *The Cultural Complex: Contemporary Jungian Perspectives on Psyche and Society*. London: Routledge.

Squire, C. (1994). Safety, danger and the movies: Women's and men's narratives of aggression. *Feminism & Psychology, 4*: 547–570.

Storr, A. (1970). *Human Aggression*. Harmondsworth: Penguin.

Tacey, D. (2012). Jung and sociology. On-line discussion group of the International Association for Jungian Studies, 29 June. http://jungianstudies. org/iajs-online-discussion-forum/.

Thomas, K. (1983). *Man and the Natural World: Changing Attitudes in England 1500–1800*. London: Allen Lane.

Totton, N. (2000). *Psychotherapy and Politics*. London: Sage.

Turkle, S. (1979). *Psychoanalytic Politics: Jacques Lacan and Freud's French Revolution*. London: Deutsch.

Walzer, M. (1983). *Spheres of Justice*. Oxford: Blackwell.

Weber, M. (1924). *The Theory of Social and Economic Organization* (Trans. A. M. Henderson & T. Parsons). New York: Free Press, 1947.

Weeks, J. (1985). *Sexuality and its Discontents*. London: Routledge.

Wilde, O. (1978). The soul of man under socialism. In: *Complete Works of Oscar Wilde*. London: Book Club Associates.

Winnicott, D. W. (1951). Transitional objects and transitional phenomena. In: M. Khan (Ed.), *Through Paediatrics to Psychoanalysis*. London: Hogarth, 1958.

Winnicott, D. W. (1963). Dependence in infant-care, in child-care, and in the psycho-analytic setting. In: M. Khan (Ed.), *The Maturational Processes and the Facilitating Environment* (pp. 249–259). London: Hogarth, 1965).

Winnicott, D. W. (1971). *Playing and Reality*. London: Tavistock.

Zaehner, R. (1957). *Mysticism: Sacred and Profane*. Oxford: Oxford University Press.

INDEX